Journal of Latinos and Education

Volume 2, Number 1, 2003

SPECIAL ISSUE
Latinos, Education, and Media

GUEST EDITORS
Xaé Alicia Reyes and Diana I. Rios

Subscriber Information: *Journal of Latinos and Education* is published four times a year by Lawrence Erlbaum Associates, Inc. Subscriptions for the 2003 volume are available on a calendar-year basis only. Full-price print subscribers to Volume 2, 2003, are entitled to receive the online version free of charge. **Full-price print** journal subscription rates are US $40 for individuals and US $195 for institutions within the United States, and US $70 for individuals and US $225 for institutions outside the United States. **Online-only** subscriptions are US $175 for institutions. **Print-only** subscriptions are US $175 for institutions within the United States, and US $205 for institutions outside the United States.

Send subscription orders, information requests, and address changes to the Journal Subscription Department, Lawrence Erlbaum Associates, Inc., 10 Industrial Avenue, Mahwah, NJ 07430–2262. Address changes should include the mailing label or a facsimile. Claims for missing issues cannot be honored beyond 4 months after mailing date. Duplicate copies cannot be sent to replace issues not delivered due to failure to notify publisher of change of address.

This journal is abstracted or indexed in *Current Index to Journals in Education; EBSCO*host *Products;* and *ERIC Clearinghouse on Rural Education and Small Schools (ERIC/CRESS)*. Microform copies of this journal are available through ProQuest Information and Learning, P.O. Box 1346, Ann Arbor, MI 48106–1346. For more information, call 1–800–521–0600 x2888.

JOURNAL OF LATINOS AND EDUCATION, 2(1), 1

An Introduction to This Special Thematic Issue

Bienvenidos,

Welcome to the first issue of Volume 2 of the *Journal of Latinos and Education* (*JLE*).

The idea for this special thematic issue first began during Spring 2001, when the Puerto Rican and Latino Studies Institute (PRLS) called together a small group of scholars to the University of Connecticut campus in Storrs for intense discussions on contemporary issues facing U.S. Latinos. Scholars presented "thought" pieces on topics that included globalization, law, education, and communication. The participating audience was engaged in a provocative dialogue, and the need for further elaboration emerged. Soon afterward, we began the process of assembling the following contributions.

We envisioned a collection that would speak to scholars, educators, students, administrators, and policymakers concerned with advancing knowledge in critical education, language policy and the press, technology and education policy, selective skills in media reception, and critical analysis of popular television programming. A potential special thematic issue of *JLE* blossomed into "LATINOS, EDUCATION, AND MEDIA," a thoughtful tome written with cross-disciplinarians in mind.

This special issue of *JLE* has brought together a number of us who are located throughout academic areas of specialization. We also have broken with the sections that regularly appear in this journal. Our desire is that the following contributions will inspire and provoke positive action at the broad intersections of Education and Media.

Thank you—*gracias*.

Xaé Alicia Reyes and Diana I. Rios
Guest Editors

JOURNAL OF LATINOS AND EDUCATION, 2(1), 3–11

Imaging Teachers: In Fact and in the Mass Media

Xaé Alicia Reyes

NEAG School of Education and Puerto Rican & Latino Studies Institute
University of Connecticut, Storrs

Diana I. Rios

Department of Communication Sciences and Puerto Rican & Latino
Studies Institute
University of Connecticut, Storrs

The impact of mass media on teaching and on knowledge about teachers and students is considered in the dialogue between an educational researcher and a mass media researcher. The discussion points to the need for critical analysis of printed news reports, newscasts, television, and film and representations of teachers and students. The stereotypes in films and the abundance of reports on high dropout rates, and low academic achievement of Latina/os, impact teachers and the general public, who often view negative images as absolute truths. The inclusion of a critique of the curriculum and conversations within communities is necessary to separate fact from fiction.

Key words: teachers, students, representations, Latinas, Latinos, stereotypes, mass media

If you try running this school with ideas you'll have riots. Fear is what they understand. (Principal to new teacher in the 1967 film *Up the Down Staircase* [Mulligan]; Keroes, 1999, p. 53)

The constructions of the "other" in the realm of education are not produced in a vacuum, but are part of an ever-evolving process of messages shared by sociocultural and economic agents. The "other" can be a person or cultural representative who is "packaged" to appear to us as unknown, curious, or strange in some way. The ef-

---

Requests for reprints should be sent to Xaé Alicia Reyes, Neag School of Education U–2033, University of Connecticut Storrs, Storrs, CT 06269. E-mail: xreyes@uconn.edu

fects of mediated constructions are not inconsequential in how society perceives key actors in education, that is the educators themselves and the students with whom they engage. Gripping photographs in newspapers, alluring depictions of people and locales in news reports, soap operas, infotainment and prime time shows, films, videos, and digital video disks (DVD) are pervasive. Several scholars have critically discussed one or more issues in the social constructions of race, ethnicity, gender, and class in print and broadcast news and television entertainment (Berger & Luckman, 1966; Giroux, 1994; Gitlin, 1980; Press & Cole, 1999; Tuchman, 1978).

Overall, it can be said that mass media hold important roles in forming constructions of the "other" in the public mind. Of specific concern in this article are the mediated constructions of the teacher as the other, and the intersections of ethnicity, race, and gender in the creations of this other. We will discuss how the teacher other is placed in predictable contexts infused with elements of drama, comedy, and romantic tension; these are contexts of teacher–student, teacher–colleague, teacher–school, teacher–community, and teacher–society.

Regarding real world teachers in general, it should not be a surprise that the public is offered a warped repertoire of what a teacher is. Regarding Latina/o educators in the real world specifically, we conclude that the public again is left with sparse ingredients from which to make realistic assumptions, perceptions, or interpretations about what a Latina/o teacher is or can be. Though there are some exceptions, mediated manifestations of the teaching profession are more often problematic and dangerous than inspiring and honorable.

The clash between real or factual knowledge about the "other" and media (re)created knowledge prompts a critical analysis and dialogue between the world of an educator and education researcher (Reyes) and an educator and communication researcher (Rios). Both have had long-term and repeated exposure to mass mediated constructions of many others. Through dialogue, we support a critical awareness and healthy skepticism about mass mediated creations of the teacher as other that are made to be memorable, of high ratings, and economically successful.

CRITICAL VIEWING IN K–12 AND HIGHER EDUCATION

The debate on who should teach values and whose values are taught delays the implementation of a core curriculum where there may be a critical analysis of how the media influences beliefs and values of our society. This analysis might illuminate the understandings we have about who gets to teach and why some, particularly students of color, fail to identify with the teaching profession. We could also benefit from the analysis of who is viewed and depicted as an achiever and who is not.

Xaé Reyes: There is a dangerous intermingling of fact and fiction with regard to the teaching profession that may affect our expectations about real educators. We may gather assumptions and have interpretation of realities through those provided to us by the media. In spite of numerous efforts to infuse the general K–12 curriculum with course work or entire courses that address media literacy and educate students in habits that involve critical viewing (Golden, 2001), the adoption is still tied to media studies or curricula for performing arts magnets. This limited approach dismisses the importance of a critique that will allow students to distinguish between fact and fiction and assist them in creating and rejecting false representations of otherness.

In communities where there is limited contact with diverse populations or where travel abroad is a distant reality, there is a reliance or dependency on the tube to inform and glean information about the outside world. Henry Giroux's *Disturbing Pleasures* (1994) deconstructs a number of films and opens our eyes to a completely different interpretation of the representations we may have innocently enjoyed. It is almost impossible to ever look at a film again without questioning its authenticity and impact on our perceptions and construction of meaning. As we struggle with this, we must acknowledge that many of our experiences and interactions have already been affected by the absence of a critique in educational settings.

How many of these situations are related to the abundant depictions of minorities in these situations through press reports of testing outcomes or the abundance of films reinforcing these images? In contrast, the Columbine incidents presented a reality that challenged the stereotypes perpetuated by the media as well as the paradigms of successful suburban mainstream students.

There is an issue of intentionality involved in biased reporting or creative interpretations of realities for entertainment purposes. In both cases we need to engage in an analysis of intended or nonintended consequences. The common warning "do not try this at home" seems appropriate when dealing with these scenarios that affect life in schools and teacher student relationships. What appears to happen is a domino effect; the report of an event, such as inappropriate relationships between teachers and students, spawns book contracts, movie deals, and a sequel of similar reports that continues to feed the frenzy and sensation surrounding the case. As a result, teacher–student relationships come under scrutiny. It's as if the media needs to seize the momentum to the detriment of authentic and legitimate behaviors between caring teachers and their students as these are assigned negative connotations. One wonders if the influence of media representations and ethical considerations are part of media studies.

Diana Rios: In my professional experiences, many undergraduate students who declare majors in mass communication in higher education would like to learn production and copy writing skills that they can use for a career in media right after completing their bachelor's degree. These graduates are the future media professionals who will be in front of and behind the camera. These will become the talent, creative minds, market planners, and managers in the next generation of the industry. A few students, those who will go to graduate school, declare a communication major wanting to hone critical, analytical, and reasoning skills as well as practical skills. Though all students have different goals, and no two departments or schools of communication are the same, all students of communication will finish with a more sophisticated knowledge of the impact of mass communication and all should have developed better critical media reception skills. One of the first things they learn is that there is not one media effects theory; there are many theories. Scholars choose a few on which to specialize and build their careers with original investigations, writing, teaching, and speaking about the media effects theories that they themselves find most compelling. Overall, individuals who major in communication have learned the classic theories of communication and journalism and can use this higher education in the media profession or other professions. This is not to say that noncommunication students in higher education are not more susceptible to mediated impact simply because they were not communication majors. They, of course, complete their education with other kinds of analytical reasoning abilities and preparation.

EDUCATORS NOT EXEMPT FROM MEDIA IMPACT

It is important to remember that we are our genders, our ethnic groups, our personal lives, and our professional selves. Thus we experience the same vulnerability to over-exposure to images and stereotypes as everyone else. These images have an impact on how we see ourselves in those representations and may, in fact, affect our self-concept and the way we feel others see us.

XR: Teachers in our communities are not exempt from influences of mediated constructions. Although on an intellectual level they are exposed to concrete information about cultural practices, values, and beliefs of populations that do not resemble them, they are influenced by the depictions that appear to bring these "characters" to life. Thus we must constantly question our responses to others and wonder how much of what we presuppose is based on fictional characters and how much on first-hand interactions. Along with this we must constantly remind ourselves that we are first and foremost individuals and no group is totally homogenous. If our interactions in classrooms are guided by the principle of seeing each of our students as an individual, prejudiced views will not prevail. We can encourage students and our communities to be vigilant in reacting to these patterns in reporting and in designing policy.

A number of incidents I have been privy to are examples of these stereotypical notions. A recent conversation with a staff member of a local school in a predominantly Latina/o setting brought about a discussion of the need for the breakfast program. The person stated that this was a bad program because it "enabled the lazy mothers to stay in bed rather than getting up to fix breakfast for the children." I argued that the majority of the parents worked in custodial, factory, nursing home, or farm jobs where they had to leave their homes long before the children were off to school and that this was a legitimate rationale for a breakfast program. Another situation is related to the issue of mobility. Some teachers complain constantly about children entering and exiting schools during the academic year. They make judgements as to the sense of responsibility and emphasis on schooling, or lack thereof, of the parents. These teachers lack understanding of seasonal work, landlord–tenant issues, extended families as support systems, and other situations that dictate the need to move. In some of these cases, programming such as the "American Family" (Nava, 2002) would enlighten some as they observe an aunt as the next door neighbor, grandparents raising their grandchild, and other authentically represented situations.

Another approach to addressing the distorted images is the use of documentaries such as *The First Year* (Guggenheim, 2001), where one can see the difficulties faced by teachers in urban settings. This documentary shows real people and the teachers often relate to students' behaviors based on their own experiences. One particular case shows an English as a second language teacher. She shares her stories of fighting for her rights in order to get the students organized to testify at a hearing to avoid budget cuts that can eliminate their programs. This perspective is missing in commercial television and even in press reports.

DR: In the present information age, mediated communication is playing a bigger role in people's lives. What had been predicted decades ago regarding the growth and use of newer technologies is a present day reality. Because mediated communication used in developed nations is pervasive and inescapable, the public needs to pay even more attention to increasing their critical abilities in media selection and use.

There are many qualities of newer media that have allowed for flexibility in use and expedient access. However, we as a society should not become so enamoured by the new channels of communication that we do not wish to be more active and critical when we read, listen to, and view mediated representations. It is important to say that publics with formal education and educators of all levels are not exempt from potential impact of the mass media, although they have more schooling than others. There are many scholarly perspectives about the abilities of people to sort out the information that they are exposed to. Media uses and gratifications theory says that people are active users of the media and posits that people are not dupes with easily maleable minds. People choose media to fulfill various utilitarian needs. Theories of selective perception, selection, and retention also describe how people differ in the ways they receive communication messages (McQuail, 1987).

As part of understanding the potential of media impact in a society, we must also consider the menu from which media audiences must choose. The menus have expanded in their forms; there are larger quantities of programming, but how much of the content has changed? Continued economic pressures for quickly made productions, high commercial value, and broad appeal have still lead to over reliance on narrative formulas and character types. For example, the character types of Latinos and ethnic/racial "others" in news and entertainment media are still reminiscent of the types found in previous cycles in film, television, and radio. We still find the "sexy señorita," "the virgin," "the suffering mother," "the greaser," "the bandit," and many other iterations of these types (Berg, 1990; Carstarphen & Rios, in press; Keller, 1994). These ever-repeated Hollywood constructions are internationally disseminated. Repetitive mass media images have the chance to gradually influence public's perspectives and attitudes about people, topics, and issues over time according to cultivation theory (McQuail, 1987).

I was disappointed to see a gang of male student youths represented in the film *Pay it Forward* (Leder, 2000), which otherwise has excellent social messages. The ethnic and racial identification of the gang members was not verbally stated but visual cues were all too clear. The swarthiness of the rough boys, the style of dress, and a brandished switchblade indicated that the boys that bullied and finally killed the European American boy Trevor McKinney (played by Haley Joel Osment) were Latino *cholos* "gangbangers," or just plain, greasy, at-risk for drop-out, bandit types preparing for a notorious future of crime. These little gangsters would never sit in preparation workshops for standardized achievement tests. Furthermore, it pained me to think that a tremendous amount of films spit out by the Hollywood machine are what I see dominating popular movie theater marquis in Mexico City and Barcelona. The Mexicans, the Spanish, and the world view what current U.S. Latinos are up to through these general market films as well as through syndicated television shows. The educators of today, who tend to have a European American lived experience, have a lifetime of exposure to the mediated constructions of cultural, ethnic, and racial others. In real life these others are Latino, African American, Arab American, Asian, and American Indian students. The educators of tomorrow will continue to be exposed to similar mediated and social constructions of ethnic and racial others. We must ask to what degree our country's educators have been prepared, or will be prepared, for the real "others" in their midst when a lifetime of mediated constructions about the others has been delimited.

TEACHER AS SAVIOR, STUDENT AS FAILURE

The reinforcement of stereotypes in our imaginations can inevitably affect our responses to people along limited parameters. When one considers the basic caricatures of the heroic Lone Ranger and his indigenous sidekick, the submissive Tonto, whose name translates as "simpleton," like the sleepy Mexican hiding behind the huge sombrero, this is more than evident. These are the images in the public's social constructions of people of Latina/o heritage.

XR: Another aspect involves student expectations of teachers as saviors and teacher expectations of students as incapable of succeeding based on their stereotypical expectations. These are just a few of the dynamics that result from artificially constructed notions about the "other." The only way to counter the pervasive effects of the media is to create awareness in viewers and readers so that we all develop a questioning stance and engage in discussions about validity and reliability of information vis-à-vis the factual knowledge that we may or may not be able to access.

Let us take for example the popular film *Dangerous Minds* (Smith, 1995). This film is based on the lived classroom experiences of a former U.S. Marine. The main character is a female, whose military training blends with her own personal understandings of how expectations affect student performance as well as their lives. For starters, the film embellishes the heroism of its protagonist by selecting a very attractive Michelle Pfeiffer for the lead role. The film is also selective in terms of the vignettes from the original book by Johnson (1992) called *My Posse Don't Do Homework*. It enhances the heroic antics of the protagonist and emphasizes the hopelessness in the lives of the students. Coolio's song "Gangsta's Paradise" caps off the imagery of the cool tough gorgeous teacher in a school setting that appears life threatening. The imagery does little to build positive images of urban schooling and minority students. As we assess the impact of such imagery one cannot disassociate reports on high drop-out rates among minority students, the higher truancy and suspension rates among this population, and the lower academic and testing outcomes among this population.

DR: There are too many films that offer audiences the teacher as saviors who need to rescue students from their inherent shortcomings. Most commonly the teacher is a middle class European American, who arrives on the scene with superior skills, ethics, cultural values than those of the ethnic and racial other. The best known of these pictures, featuring numerous juvenile delinquents, is *The Blackboard Jungle* (1955), directed by Richard Brooks. The best known television series of this kind was shown during the 1970s. *The White Shadow* (Paltrow, 1978–1981) was a hit prime time television series that featured a White, ex-professional basketball player as a coach in an inner-city Los Angeles high school. As the title of the show suggests, the burden of White patriarchy is to shadow, look out for, mentor, and otherwise deliver students from their non-White decrepitude. The media construction of the White racial class delivering untutored people of color is still repeated today as we see in *Finding Forrester* (Van Sant, 2000).

Our Miss Brooks (Lewis, 1956) was a popular radio and television series that captured the attention of entire families in the 1950s and 1960s. Miss Brooks lived in a proper European American neighborhood and taught at a nice European American middle class school. The film called *Our Miss Brooks* debuted in 1956, when, finally, Miss Brooks was able to catch the man she had designs on since radio comedy days. My over 60-year-old father, now a retired educator, recalled Miss Brooks on radio, television, and film vividly. He explained to me that she was always after a particular, bright, male colleague who could never pick up on her verbal cues of romantic interest. He recalled Miss Brooks as being able to communicate with subtle witticisms and sometimes with witticisms that were not too subtle.

The naive teacher Miss Sylvia Barrett of *Up the Down Staircase* (Mulligan, 1967) was also quite proper. Walking the hallways in conservative dress, she appears as a representative of liberal, yet conventional, European American middle class values. Miss Barrett maintains her courteous demeanor and sense of humor even in the face of the inner-city structural deterioration, ethnic diversity, and violence in Spanish Harlem. Jennifer Lopez's teacher role of Miss Marquez in *Jack* (Coppola, 1996) continues to preserve female school teacher, primness, virginality, and thus morality in a middle class European American setting.

When examining the students of the prim or naive teacher, we note a contrast in most cases, but not all. The students of the Miss Brooks' world are not violent, needy, people of color. They are gregarious, middle-class European Americans without serious worries, similar to the kids in Miss Marquez's class in the film *Jack*. The nice middle-class students are not predisposed to malicious mischief, assault, murder, or suicide. These are traits we see among the working poor and working class ethnic Americans and students of color in *The Blackboard Jungle* (Brooks, 1955), *Up the Down Staircase* (Mulligan, 1967), *Cooley High* (Schultz, 1975), *Lean on Me* (Avildsen, 1989), and *The Substitute* (Mandel, 1996).

CONCLUDING REMARKS

There is a combination of factors that can lead to a critical consciousness in our society. This critical consciousness in turn allows us to further educate ourselves and others, and also allows us to develop the ability to separate fact from fiction. We have a number of serious and talented actors, such as Edward James Olmos and Esai Morales, who have been very vocal in their rejection of roles that perpetuate negative stereotypes. We have committed organizations such as the National Association of Latino Independent Producers (NALIP) who are an important part of the future of remade Latino images through new media productions and Latino writing and acting opportunities. We have organizations like Nosotros and the Puerto Rican Legal Defense and Education Fund (PRLDEF) that take initiatives to promote better Latina/o news coverage and prime time television images. Teachers who gain awareness about media stereotyping can discuss their pervasiveness and disallow media influences in classrooms, schools, and communities. A willingness to enter dialogues about the social impact of the mass media is an imperative for all of us.

REFERENCES

Avildsen, J. G. (Director). (1989). *Lean on me* [Motion picture]. United States: Warner.

Berg, C. R. (1990). Stereotyping in film in general with Hispanics in particular. *Howard Journal of Communication, 2,* 286–300.

Berger, P., & Luckman, T. (1966). *The social construction of reality: A treatise in the sociology of knowledge.* New York: Doubleday.

Brooks, R. (Director). (1955). *The blackboard jungle* [Motion picture]. United States: MGM.

Carstarphen, M. G., & Rios, D. I. (in press). Brown and Black women in Nancy Savoca's "The 24-Hour Woman." In D. I. Rios. & A. Mohamed (Eds.), *Brown and Black communication: Latino and African American conflict and convergence in mass media.* Westport, CT: Greenwood.

Coolio. (1995). Gangsta's paradise. Tommy Boy Records.

Coppola, F. F. (Director). (1996). *Jack* [Motion picture]. United States: Hollywood Pictures.

Giroux, H. (1994). *Disturbing pleasures: Learning popular culture.* New York: Routledge.

Gitlin, T. (1980). *The whole world is watching: Mass media in the making and unmaking of the New Left.* Berkeley: University of California Press.

Golden, J. (2001). *Reading in the dark: Using film as a tool in the English classroom.* Urbana, IL: National Council of Teachers of English.

Guggenheim, D. (Director). (2001). *The first year* [Television]. Los Angeles: PBS Teachers Documentary Project.

Johnson, L. (1992). *My posse don't do homework.* New York: St. Martin's.

Keller, G. D. (1994). *Hispanics and United States film: An overview and handbook.* Tempe, AR: Bilingual/Review Press.

Keroes, J. (1999). *Tales out of school: Gender, longing, and the teacher in fiction and film.* Carbondale, IL: Southern Illinois.

Leder, M. (Director). (2000). *Pay it forward* [Motion picture]. United States: Warner.

Lewis, A. (Director). (1956). *Our Miss Brooks* [Television series]. United States: Warner.

Mandel, R. (Director). *The substitute* [Motion picture]. United States: Orion.

McQuail, D. (1987). *Mass communication theory: An introduction.* Newbury Park, CA: Sage.

Mulligan, R. (Director). (1967). *Up the down staircase* [Motion picture]. United States: Warner.

Nava, G. (Executive Producer/Director). (2002). *American family* [Television series]. Hollywood: KCET and Twentieth Century Fox Films Corp.

Paltrow, B. (Executive Producer). (1978–1981). *The white shadow* [Television series]. CBS.

Press, A. L., & Cole, E. R. (1999). *Speaking of abortion: Television and authority in the lives of women.* Chicago: University of Chicago Press.

Schultz, M. (Director). (1975). *Cooley high* [Motion picture]. United States: American International Pictures.

Smith, J. N. (Director). (1995). *Dangerous minds* [Motion picture]. United States: Hollywood Pictures.

Tuchman, G. (1978). *Making news: A study in the construction of reality.* New York: Free Press.

Van Sant, G. (Director). (2000). *Finding Forrester* [Motion picture]. United States: Columbia Pictures.

JOURNAL OF LATINOS AND EDUCATION, 2(1), 13–21

Missing in Action: Reconstructing Hope and Possibility Among Latino Students Placed at Risk

Maria D. Martinez

The Center for Academic Programs
University of Connecticut

Latino students are noticeably underrepresented in post-secondary education. Their inability to access critical information about educational opportunities has resulted in low numbers of students gaining admission to colleges and universities, particularly 4-year institutions. The lack of preparation and support in their journey to earn a college degree can prove to be a challenging one given their academic histories. The educational opportunity program described here serves students who meet one or more of these factors: 1st-generation college students, low-income, demographically underrepresented, and identified as having the need for additional academic support services for college level work.

Key words: Latino students, TRIO programs, parent involvement, first-generation, low-income, low expectations, academic, support services, at risk

The role of my high school teachers was minimal. I cannot recall specific examples of teachers encouraging or motivating me personally to attend an institution of higher education. My guidance counselor, for example, felt that I should not attend any four year institution. (Javier Padilla, interviewee)

Like Javier, many of us have been taught that education is the key to success. We have been told that if we work hard, we will be rewarded and therefore we can aspire to a better quality of life for our family and ourselves. Unfortunately, the reality is that even when we work hard, we do not necessarily get the expected results. The journey through unfriendly or insensitive school systems can be a challenge. The

---

Requests for reprint should be sent to Maria D. Martinez, University of Connecticut, 341 Mansfield Road, Storrs, CT 06269. E-mail: capadm06@uconnrm.uconn.edu

low expectations placed on Latinos and other students of color impact their relationships with school officials and their ability to navigate the systems successfully. The attainment of a college degree is, in most cases, the expectation for all middle-class White Americans. Many researchers have confirmed that individuals who come from an educated, middle-class household are more likely to participate in post-secondary education and be successful in that endeavor (Hossler, Schmit, & Vesper, 1999; Perna, 2000). Conversely, studies have revealed that students who come from families with lower incomes are less likely than other students to plan for higher education (Hossler, Braxton, & Coopersmith, 1989; Kane, 1994; Kane & Spizman, 1994; Manski & Wise, 1983; Rouse, 1994). Additionally, researchers have established the correlation between income, education, and success in post-secondary education. According to Thomas G. Mortenson, policy analyst with the Post-secondary Education OPPORTUNITY and senior scholar with The Pell Center for the Study of Opportunity in Higher Education, college graduation is determined at birth. He affirms that only 1 in 12 children from low-income families with noncollege educated parents will have a bachelor's degree by age 24. Studies confirm that having a college education signifies a higher probability of a better quality of life for any individual. Consequently, the high drop out rates among Latinos increase their probabilities of living in poverty. The poverty rate among Latinos in 1999 was 22.8%, which statistically equaled the rate in 1979, the all time low (Census, 2000).

The academic outcomes and the remarkable increase in the Latino population challenge the policies and practices of traditional models of education. Latinos now represent almost 10% of the total student enrollment in higher education. They comprise 14.5% of the traditional college-age population in the United States, a proportion expected to rise to 22% by 2025 (ERIC Digest 162, p. 2). Although there have been increases in the completion of high school and attendance to post-secondary institutions by Latinos, the rate of growth has remained at the same. There has been no consistent progression among Latinos. According to the National Center for Education Statistics, "Hispanic students are more likely than White students to leave school before completing a high school program. Hispanics are the fastest growing group in the nation's elementary and secondary schools." As we are all very aware, the problem begins at the K–12 level. While 90% of non-Latino students are completing secondary schools nationwide, only 60% of the Latino students are doing so. The problem is highly concentrated in some of the major cities in the nation (Flores, 1999).

When we focus on income, a case can be made that for many Latino students the economic uncertainties coupled with the lack of information about educational opportunities can impact their desire or willingness to pursue a college degree. Many Latino students do not get the appropriate advising about the numerous resources available to individuals interested in pursuing a college education. Discussions about financial aid programs, scholarships, and other means of paying for college are in many cases reserved for students who demonstrate ability with traditional measures, such as SAT scores (Darder, Torres, & Gutieerez, 1997, p. 339). The low expectations emerged as an important theme in interviews conducted with Latino university graduates for this article. Their responses confirm that many Latino students are still singled out early in the educational process as not having the aspiration and/or the ability to conquer the rigors of a college experience. As a result, a significant number of children resign themselves to mediocrity and internalize a sense of failure before an attempt is made to be successful. Their responses also describe successful strategies such as high school enrichment programs, pre-college or bridge programs, tutoring, mentoring, peer advising, and other programs can serve as conduits for the rebuilding of self-confidence and academic preparation, as well as to instill motivation.

THE STUDY

In this article, portions of data collected in an ongoing larger study of students who were subjected to low expectations and, in some cases, denied access to opportunities available to mainstream students are examined. The reader will find responses to open ended-interviews from a series of case studies that are part of a larger project. Students' personal accounts of their experiences provide valuable insights into their educational processes. Researchers have begun to realize that human feeling does not pollute understanding (Eisner, 1997). The four students included in this article shared important information about interactions with teachers and other school officials. Their perceptions regarding the opportunities denied them and the obstacles they confronted before attending college revealed the extent of reconstruction of academic self-confidence needed to help them navigate the higher education setting. The emergent themes chosen for this discussion are closely related to stereotypical expectations often reinforced by media images of Latinos. As we know, and as these data confirm, many educators operate under these assumptions.

In the following pages, four former participants of a TRIO[1] Student Support Service Program (SSS), Javier, Angel, Noemí, and Lynnette, discuss situations that may have obstructed their quest for higher education. The stories of these individuals differ from each other in many ways; nevertheless the common denomina-

---

[1]TRIO encompasses a series of programs established by Congress to help low-income Americans enter college, graduate, and move on to participate more fully in America's economic and social life. These Programs are funded under Title IV of the Higher Education Act of 1965 and are referred to as the TRIO Programs (initially just three programs). SSS helps low-income students to stay in college until they earn their baccalaureate degrees. Among other services participants receive tutoring, counseling, and academic enrichment.

tor is their experience with a program that provided the educational opportunity to prepare them to succeed in higher education.

Description of Interviewees

All four interviewees are Latinos who participated in a pre-college program that supported their admission to a university under the auspices of a TRIO program. They met some, but not all, of the requirements to be admitted to the university under regular admissions criteria. All four students possessed academic records where college-related curriculum was nonexistent, nor had their schools addressed their social and affective needs adequately.

Student interviews shed light on the issues that framed their desire to attend college: the influence of their parents; the low expectations placed on them by their teachers and others; the inability of the system to provide proper advice; subsequent identification for participation in TRIO programs; and identification of their own potential to be successful and the strategies needed to reach their goals.

EMERGING THEMES

Parent Involvement

Although the majority of the parents in our study had very little knowledge or experience regarding college admissions and the college process in general, the individuals selected for this article coincide in their appreciation of the consistent encouragement from their parents to attend college. Parents of the interviewees were not the typical White, majority parent. They did not participate in any formalized parent groups in the schools, such as PTO. Nonetheless, the interest in their child's education was consistently demonstrated by their words of encouragement and the numerous attempts to help or assist with the homework and school projects.

> Javier: The basic idea inculcated was the notion that education was the key to success and necessary to avoid blue-collar work. It was made clear that more than a high school education was required. However, deciphering the difference between a high school education and a college education was virtually obsolete. I don't think my parents understood what was required to obtain a formal education. They certainly did not understand the process involved in attending a post-secondary institution. However, there was no doubt and it was made very clear that a formal education beyond high school was necessary although the type of education and how to obtain it was not clear.

Angel: My parents always thought a college education was necessary to live well. …
In my head, I always told myself that I could do nothing else but go to college if I
wanted to make it.

Lynnette: Both my parents spoke to me about continuing my education, especially my
mother. She always says, "Si yo tuviera tu edad y estuviera soltera, yo estudiaria todo
lo posible y me pasaria viajando" (If I were your age and single, I would study every-
thing possible and spend my time traveling). My mother and father are divorced, and
so my mother has not only motivated me in gaining my education, but has also supported me financially when I needed books and supplies.

These statements by our interviewees are consistent with findings published in *The
Chronicle of Higher Education* on June 1, 2001. "The study found that 65% of Hispanic parents compared to 47% of Black parents and 33% of White parents, believe
that a college education is the single most important factor to an individual's success" (p. 13).

Low Expectations

The issue of low expectations and the self-fulfilling prophecy effect is well docu-
mented in the literature. According to Darder (1991) teacher expectations that are
related to lower class and bicultural students can result in teachers being more
likely to hold negative expectations for these students rather than for middle class
White children (p. 18). These expectations are extended to other members of the educational setting such as guidance counselors. Our students' remarks on this issue
are very telling.

Javier: My guidance counselor, for example, felt very strongly that I should not attend
any 4-year institution for that matter. … A second incident comes to mind in which I
asked a teacher if I could go to the library to complete a scholarship application and he
indicated that it was a waste of my time.

Noemí: On my own I decided to apply for college late in my senior year sort of like a
shot in the dark because I didn't have any options after high school. I did the work myself and hoped for the best.

Lynnette: The major challenge I confronted was not feeling completely prepared for
college, compared to students who were in the Classical Magnet Program.

As Fine (1991) stated, "Students who begin with the greatest economic disadvan-
tages receive the least enriching educations and end up with fewer, less valuable
and historically deflating diplomas" (p. 26). Our students' voices are a reflection of

these patterns that eventually keep them out of 4-year institutions and in the worst cases lead to dropping out of school.

Transition to College Life

Once on campus students became aware of their academic needs. They also knew the amount of work that was needed to succeed in college. As Javier explained, "I quickly learned that in order to compete with classmates I had to study twice as much, and I had a lot of 'catching up' to do. I did not receive all of the basic educational concepts to compete successfully."

> Lynnette: My challenge in college was balancing my personal life and school. Another challenge was trying to let go of those bad study habits.

In all of the cases, success in college was attributed to the determination to obtain a degree and to the assistance provided by the educational opportunity program in which they had participated while in college. They realized early on in their college career that they were competing with many students who had been fortunate to come from more advanced school systems that had many more resources for their students. Unlike the interviewees' experiences, these students came from higher income backgrounds, and enjoyed their families' support as most of the parents were college graduates themselves. It wasn't about whether or not they were going to college but rather what college or university they were planning to attend.

> Angel: I think determination helped me stay in school as well as family and friends.
> Lynnette: The SSS advisors always wanted me to strive for my potential abilities. They told me that I could do it; that I could succeed, and not only that, but they expected me to do so.

This last remark reflects that the value of high expectations is significant in helping students realize their potential. Institutional commitment to students is identified in the literature as being critical to retention (McInnis, James, & Hartley, 2000). Surveys of students withdrawing from courses suggests that those who feel isolated or disconnected from the institution are more likely to withdraw than those who feel connected to the institution and its occupants (Peel, 2000; Tinto, 1995; Tinto, Goodsell-Love, & Russo, 1993).

Support Services Making a Difference

The students interviewed for this article emphasized the importance of having a connection to the university through their participation in the SSS TRIO program.

They all remember their SSS counselor and speak very highly of that person. They viewed the precollegiate experience as a wonderful opportunity to be introduced to the rigors of college work. They also discussed the advantages of having a connection with the program and their SSS peers, and the fact that knowing other students as a freshman helped immensely with their adjustment to campus.

> Noemí: I must give credit to my SSS advisor … who encouraged me and gave me guidance along the way.

> Lynnette: The main support came from the SSS program. Another source of support were my friends; some were connected to SSS one way or another. All of them knew the importance of gaining a higher education and this created a form of support and motivation for each other.

According to a study by Tinto, Goodsell-Love, and Russo (1993), students who felt ignored by lecturers and were inhibited about contacting them, even about academic issues, wound up withdrawing from college and described staff as "uncaring and indifferent to the needs of the students." This points to the need for institutions to establish connections with enrolling students (Tinto, Goodsell-Love, & Russo, 1993).

Role Models: An Important Variable

None of the students profiled for this article experienced finding a person they can consider a role model or mentor throughout their K–12 education. One student talks about the influence one Spanish teacher had in her life as an isolated event. Another student makes reference to a mentorship relationship he had with an individual through a community mentoring program. In some cases they described the positive impact such connections had in their lives and how it helped and provided guidance. In other instances, the absence of these types of relationships/connections was clearly a factor that prevented the students from accessing important information regarding the college process. Research has affirmed the critical need for bilingual and ethnic teachers to serve as role models (Flores & Clark, 1997). As Noemí stated, "I did not get to socialize much or converse frequently with teachers (they did not get a chance to know me). My senior year of high school I did have one teacher who realized my potential and encouraged me to continue with my education and to do something with my life."

CONCLUSIONS

The students interviewed here describe repeated instances of inequity in schools based on assumptions regarding Latino students and their academic potential. According to their experiences, misinformation, and/or lack of adequate advising, a peer culture where the majority of students of color are relegated to a less challenging curriculum, all presented obstacles to access to higher education. "Conflicting obligations, false expectations, and lack of preparation are among the factors that may hinder their success" (Access, 1996). Despite the conflicting nature of some of the literature, our interviewees' statements point to the need for institutions to provide adequate student support services in ways that students feel comfortable accessing them. Support services, such as academic skill advising, counseling, medical services, financial advice, as well as equity advocacy, are vital resources for students experiencing difficulties, particularly in the 1st year (Promnitz & Germain, 1996). Unlike higher socioeconomic status, college-bound students, the typical SSS student arrives on campus with a set of expectations that, in most cases, do not match the services available in many institutions. Programs described by the interviewees here provide the necessary services and interventions to help students complete college.

> Over 1,900 TRIO programs currently serve nearly 700,000 low-income Americans between the ages of 11 and 27. Thirty-nine percent of TRIO students are White, 36% are African-American, 16% are Hispanic, 5% are Native American, and 4% are Asian American. Sixteen thousand TRIO students are disabled. (www.trioprograms.org)

Although TRIO efforts are reaching a significant number of low-income and first-generation students, only a fraction of Hispanics (16%) are being served. The participation of Latino students in educational opportunity programs is noticeably lower than that of other groups. This presents a problem in light of the 2000 Census, which show the Hispanic population growing at an astounding rate. It is incumbent on those of us who are familiar and/or have benefited from these programs to disseminate the information to our communities, especially to Latinos of low-income first-generation college-student backgrounds.

REFERENCES

Access. (1996). Improving diversity in student recruitment and retention, understanding and assisting the first-generation student (Vol. iv). Cedar Rapids, IA: Author.
Darder, A. (1991). *Culture and power in the classroom.* Wesport, CT: Bergin & Garvey.
Darder, A., Torres, R., & Gutieerez, H. (1997). *Latinos and education: A critical reader.* New York: Routledge.
Eisner, E. (1997). The promise and perils of alternative forms of data representation. *Educational Researcher, 26*(6), 4–10.
ERIC Digest Number 162. (2001). *Latinos in school: Some facts and findings* (ERIC digest 2001-02-00 ED449288, p. 2). New York: ERIC Clearinghouse on Urban Education.
Fine, M. (1991). *Framing dropouts: notes on the politics of an urban public high school.* Albany, NY: State University of New York Press.

Flores, A. (1999). Annual conference a great success. *The voice of Hispanic higher education, hispanic association of colleges and universities.* San Antonio, TX 8(12) 4.

Flores, B. B., & Clark, E. R. (1997). High –stakes testing: Barriers for prospective bilingual teachers. *Bilingual Research Journal, 21,* 335–358.

Hossler, D., Braxton, J., & Coopersmith, G. (1989). Understanding student college choice. In J. C. Smart (Ed.), *Higher education: Handbook of theory and research* (Vol. V, pp. 231–288). New York: Agathon.

Hossler, D., Schmit, J., & Vesper, N. (1999). *College to college: How social, economic, and educational factors influence the decisions students make.* Baltimore, MD: Johns Hopkins University Press.

Kane, T. J. (1994). College entry by Blacks since 1970: The role of college costs, family background, and the returns to education. *Journal of Political Economy, 102,* 878–911.

Kane, J., & Spizman, L. M. (1994). Race, financial aid awards, and college attendance: Parents and geography matter. *American Journal of Economics and Sociology, 53*(1), 73–97.

Manski, C. F., & Wise, D. A. (1983). *College choice in America.* Cambridge, MA: Harvard University Press.

McInnis, C., James, R., & Hartley, R. (2000). Trends in the first year experience in Australian universities. Department of Education, Training, and Youth Affairs (Australia).

Mortenson, T. G. (2001, October). Family income and higher education. *Postsecondary Education OP-PORTUNITY, Research letter number 112.* Oskaloosa, IA: Family Income and Higher Education Opportunity 1970 to 2000.

National Center for Education Statistics Analysis Report. (1995). *Droupout rates in the United States.*

Peel, M. (2000). Nobody cares: The challenge of isolation in school to university transition. *Journal of Institutional Research, 9*(1), 22–34.

Perna, L. W. (2000, April). *Racial/ethnic group differences in the realization of educational plans.* Paper presented at the annual conference of the American Educational Research Association, New Orleans, LA.

Promnitz, J., & Germain, C. (1996). *Student support services and academic outcomes: Achieving positive outcomes.* Retrieved May 8, 2002, from http://www.detya.gov.au/highered/eippubs/student/eip910.htm

Rouse, C. E. (1994). What to do after high school: The two-year versus four-year college enrollment decision. In R. G. Ehrenberg (Ed.), *Choices and consequences: Contemporary policy issues in education* (pp. 59–88). New York: IRL.

Tienda, M., & Simonelli, S. (2001). The chronicle of higher education: Hispanic students are missing from diversity debates. Retrieved April 22, 2002, from http://web.lexis-nexis.com/universe/doc…v&_md5=ac1a02762e5a9c5c699805405b1987c.html

Tinto, V. (1995). Learning communities, collaborative learning, and the pedagogy of educational citizenship. *AAHE Bulletin, 47,* 11–13.

Tinto, V., Goodsell-Love, A., & Russo, P. (1993). Building community among new college students. *Liberal Education, 79,* 16–21.

United States Census 2000. (2001). *Poverty in the United States: 2000.* Washington, DC: United States Census Bureau.

JOURNAL OF LATINOS AND EDUCATION, 2(1), 23–30

Surviving the "Perfect Storm": Bilingual Education Policymaking in New York City

Luis O. Reyes

Hunter College
The City University of New York

This article analyzes the storm of controversy surrounding bilingual education policymaking in New York City during Winter 2000–2001. I, a participant–observer in the process, argue that a true understanding of the policy crisis requires a critical analysis of the complex forces at work in the policymaking "storm." I document how for 6 stormy months the public was awash in a swirl of research reports, newspaper headlines, editorials and op-ed pieces, and competing sets of policy recommendations. The intended "wipeout" of bilingual education by antibilingual forces was avoided by countervailing efforts on the part of bilingual education supporters. This article argues, however, that the "political storm" left these programs minimally improved and the systemic crisis facing them largely unresolved.

Key words: bilingual education, New York City, press coverage, news, media, policymaking, Ronald Unz, Rudy Giuliani

Bilingual educators and advocates in New York City will long remember Winter 2000–2001 as the winter of the "perfect bilingual storm." Between September 2000 and the end of February 2001, New York City became the temporary center of the national antibilingual education controversy. For 6 stormy months, the public in New York City was awash in a swirl of official research reports, tabloid newspaper headlines proclaiming the "failure" of bilingual education, and editorials and op-ed pieces insisting on the need to "reform" bilingual education and give parents more "choice."

This "perfect storm" brought together the hurricane-like force of three major political players. First was "Hurricane Ron"—Ronald Unz, the Silicon Valley

---

Requests for reprints should be sent to Luis O. Reyes, 230 Central Park West, New York, NY 10024. E-mail: luisoreyes@aol.com

multi-millionaire who has crusaded across the country against bilingual education. Next in line was "Hurricane Rudy"—Rudolph Giuliani, the then-Republican mayor who had created a task force in 1998 with the announced intent of limiting the number of years students remained in bilingual classes. The last of the metaphorical storms was "Hurricane Harold"—Schools Chancellor Harold O. Levy, the noneducator then leading the City's public school system.

This article seeks to describe and analyze the storm of controversy surrounding bilingual education policymaking in New York City during Winter 2000–2001. I argue that politics "swept away" public policy, obscuring in the ensuing "storm" the true dimensions of the policy dilemmas and imperatives facing bilingual/ESL education. This critical analysis may help to explain the absence of significant, new funds and programmatic reform during the 8 years of Giuliani's administration, while the population of English language learners (ELLs) was growing dramatically and the shortage of certified bilingual and ESL teachers was continuing to mount.

What was intended as a "wipeout" of bilingual education by Unz, a major "clean-up" by Mayor Giuliani, and a political compromise by Chancellor Levy, has, in fact, left programs of critical importance to almost 160,000 youngsters minimally improved and vastly undermined. Although full-scale disaster has been avoided by countervailing efforts on the part of bilingual education supporters, I would argue, necessary and comprehensive reforms have been postponed, if not ignored.

One might think that what transpired in New York City between September 2000 and the end of February 2001 was a rational policy debate, played out in gentlemanly terms in *The New York Times*, "the paper of record." Seen from the "eye of the storm," that is, the perspective of a participant–observer, what becomes clearer is that educational policymakers made decisions about bilingual education in a highly politicized environment. The maelstrom of political influences emanating from City Hall and the editorial offices of the tabloid press held greater sway than the conclusions and policy recommendations of educational researchers.

The policy "storm" surrounding the Fall 2000 release of the Board of Education's *English Language Learners (ELL) Subcommittee Research Studies Progress Report* (New York City Board of Education, September 2000) was unprecedented. Absent from much of the debate was public understanding of the systemic problems facing bilingual/ESL instruction. To date, the public resources commensurate with the size of the challenge have been equally absent.

"THE BILINGUAL STORM": INTRODUCING THE PROTAGONISTS

Mayor Giuliani first took up the issue of bilingual education policy in his "State of the City" addresses in 1998 and 1999. He described bilingual education as a failed social experiment of the 1970s and a present crisis in need of radical change. From the beginning, the mayor sent signals of his intention to dismantle or "sunset" the 1974 ASPIRA Consent Decree (*ASPIRA of New York, Inc. v. Board of Education*, 1975), the court-mandated basis for bilingual/ESL instruction in the city. In his speeches, he also publicly embraced time and language-of-instruction limitations similar to those espoused by anti-bilingual education advocate, Ronald Unz. In January of 1999, he convened a mayoral bilingual education "reform" Task Force (R.W. Giuliani, personal communication, January 19, 1999).

Ronald Unz first entered the New York City bilingual debate in 1999 flush from his June 1998 success in passing the antibilingual ballot initiative in California known as Proposition 227. He saw his English immersion initiative implemented in California in 1999. That same year, Unz spoke in New York City at the Harvard Club, under the auspices of the conservative Manhattan Institute, and announced his intention to end bilingual education in the City in 2000. He was soon to celebrate the passing of Proposition 203 in Arizona in November 2000.

Harold Levy became Schools Chancellor in January 2000 after Mayor Giuliani had engineered the ousting of his predecessor, Rudy Crew. Levy, formerly a high-ranking officer at Citibank and a New York State Regent, had never taught or administered a school system prior to his January hiring. He led the city public school system with a waiver from the State Education Commissioner. In his first 6 months, Levy studiously avoided instructional issues except for managing the expansion of summer school; and he sought to maintain amicable relations with a mayor whose three board allies had not supported his hiring in January.

The other major protagonists in the "perfect storm" included the seven members of the City Board of Education, Randy M. Mastro (a former Chief Deputy-Mayor under Giuliani, who served as the Chair of the mayor's Task Force on Bilingual Education), and an emergent pro-bilingual coalition that the author helped to develop and coordinate. This last group, the New York Bilingual/ESL Education Reform Coalition, was made up initially of ASPIRA of New York, Inc., the Puerto Rican Legal Defense and Education Fund (PRLDEF), the New York State Association for Bilingual Education (NYSABE), the New York Immigration Coalition (NYIC), the New York State Teachers of English to Speakers of Other Languages (NYSTESOL), and other language associations and ethnic community-based organizations.

I do not claim pure objectivity in the matter, having played a unique participant–observer role. As a professor at Brooklyn College, City University of New York, I was engaged in research on successful bilingual education practices in a local elementary school. I was also active in the "storm" as a bilingual education advocate and as a spokesperson for the New York Bilingual/ESL Education Reform Coalition. In fact, I served as the Director of Research and Advocacy for ASPIRA of New York from 1983 to 1990. And I was the Manhattan representative on the New York City Board of Education from 1990 to 1998. Altogether, I had almost 20 years of experience in dealing with bilingual education policy.

INTO THE STORM: THE STATUS OF BILINGUAL
EDUCATION IN THE YEAR 2000

According to the New York City Board of Education, in 2000 there were almost 160,000 students identified as limited English proficient (LEPs) or ELLs in New York City public schools (NYC Board of Education, October 2000). There were 139,695 ELLs in general education classes and about 20,000 in special education classes. Whereas 49.3% of ELLs in general education participated in bilingual classes, 50.7% participated solely in ESL classes. The three most prevalent models conducted for ELLs in New York City were transitional bilingual educational programs, free-standing ESL programs, and two-way bilingual education or dual language programs. This last program model was and is offered as an enrichment option in some elementary schools throughout the city, but serves less than 2% of ELL students.

Just how well these various programs were serving the educational needs of ELL students has continued to be a point of controversy in New York City and in the nation at large. In Fall 2000, Giuliani and Unz's antibilingual initiatives created a particularly stormy environment for the release of the City Board of Education's *English Language Learners (ELL) Subcommittee Research Studies Progress Report* (New York City Board of Education, September 2000). This *Progress Report* was actually a series of studies commissioned by the board's ELL Committee, headed by Irving Hamer, my replacement as Manhattan representative on the board and as Chair of the ELL committee. In his letter of submission of the *Progress Report* to the board and chancellor, Hamer stated,

> The system can take pride in the many successes of these [Bilingual/ESL] programs. The good news is that our *ELL students are faring better than current perceptions and depictions* [italics added]. For example, one study examined the longitudinal progress of ELLs and their performance after exiting Bilingual/ESL programs and found that mainstream students who were *formerly served in Bilingual/ESL programs scored as high or higher than the overall student population on standardized tests of reading and mathematics* [italics added]. This was particularly true of those who exited within three or four years. (I. Hamer, personal communication, September 5, 2000)

Study 4, "Examining the longitudinal progress of ELL students and their performance after exiting from bilingual/ESL programs," from the *Progress Report* (New York City Board of Education, September 2000), had concluded that

> New York City's bilingual/ESL programs have demonstrated substantial effectiveness in developing the English language proficiency of ELLs and ensuring their success in the educational mainstream. Deeper exploration of the findings reveals considerable variation in the relative success of these students and identifies subgroups of ELLs who require additional attention. (p. 17)

The major conclusions were as follows: the City's bilingual/ESL programs were especially effective for ELLs who entered in kindergarten and Grade 1; students' ability to meet the program exit criterion was associated with strong proficiency in both English and Spanish; students who entered in Grade 6 and Grade 9 took longer in exiting; consistency of programmatic approach (bilingual or ESL) appeared to be a particularly important determinant of program exit rates, that is, not alternating between bilingual and ESL from one year to the next (New York City Board of Education, September 2000, pp. 17–18).

A month later, Hamer released his Committee's policy recommendations to the board members (I. Hamer, personal communication, October 14, 2000). His recommendations were, indeed, databased. However, they completely ignored larger, systemic issues, which I had laid out in detail in testimony at a state legislative hearing (Reyes, 1999). These included the impact of the new Regents graduation requirements on ELLs and the severe shortage of permanently certified bilingual and ESL teachers; in 2000, the uncertified teacher rates stood at 26% and 14% percent, respectively, according to Chancellor Levy (2000). I had testified in September 1999 about "the need for political awareness of these complex needs, political commitment to reform bilingual and ESL programs, and public resources commensurate to the size of the problem" (p. 6). At the time, I presented 10 recommendations for action by the Board of Education and other policymakers.

Hamer, however, had to contend with pressure from Giuliani and Unz, and their allies at the board, in the mayor's Task Force, and in the tabloid press. Mastro, as Chair of the task force, sought to shape and influence the board's decision-making process. In September 2000, Mastro went on the offensive. First, he floated the mayor's favored policy positions in a Daily News op-ed column (Mastro, 2000, September 24), and through favorable columns by *The New York Times*' John Tierney (2000, October 17; 2000, December 19).

Mastro also arranged to meet behind closed doors with representatives of ASPIRA (the plaintiffs in the 1974 Consent Decree), the Puerto Rican Legal Defense and Education Fund (the plaintiffs' attorney of record), and other bilingual advocates, including myself. He sought to placate the parties stating that he was only trying to improve bilingual programs. Unbeknownst to him, bilingual advocates had obtained drafts of his Task Force's recommendations (R. M. Mastro, personal communication, September 20, 2000). The true nature of his antibilingual education agenda was evident in the negative "spin" given to the statistics in the ELL *Progress Report* as well as in specific recommendations to "sunset" the provisions of the Consent Decree and limit the allowed number of years in bilingual programs. The Task Force's statistical distortions and recommendations appeared in new stories and friendly tabloid editorials (Daily News, 2000, October 24; Holloway, 2000, October 17; Mastro, 2000, September 24).

Lastly, Mastro hurriedly convened a public hearing of the Task Force at City Hall for October 17, 2000, without formally presenting his Task Force's policy recommendations to the general public. Mastro was also privately negotiating with the chancellor to gain Levy's support for the mayor's preferred proposals. All the while, Mastro was engineering the editorial support of the *Daily News* and the *New York Post*, the major daily tabloids. The October 17th hearing led off with invited testimony by Unz followed by testimony by disgruntled Latino parents. These parents had unsuccessfully sued over allegations that their children had been coerced into staying in bilingual classes in Bushwick, Brooklyn elementary schools. At the hearing, though, the Latino parents actually stated that they supported quality bilingual programs.

I also submitted testimony, describing this as "a time of great need for English Language Learners (ELLs) and Bilingual Education in New York." (Reyes, 2000). I related the fact that the city board had received no new funds to help the City's ELL students to meet the new Regents graduation requirements. The board's Budget Office had estimated the cost of hiring the required 600 qualified ESL teachers at about $55 million (pp. 2–3). I had refined my December 1999 recommendations from 10 to 8 to reflect the growing consensus among members of the then emergent New York Bilingual/ESL Education Reform Coalition.

The Coalition members began meeting in September 2000 while each organization mobilized and responded individually to the media's distortions of the *Progress Report* findings and to the antibilingual campaign unleashed by the mayor's allies. The Coalition itself sent an open letter to the members of the Board of Education and Chancellor Levy, "as educators, community leaders, representatives of diverse language communities, and affected students and their parents" (New York Bilingual/ESL Education Reform Coalition, personal communication, October 26, 2000). The signatories, representing more than thirty organizations and other individuals, called upon the board and chancellor "to listen attentively to our concerns and recommendations, and to act upon them in a deliberative and inclusionary manner."

The Coalition's nine recommendations were in direct response to the policy proposals floated by Mastro in the newspapers (providing parents of ELL students the "choice" of a new English immersion program model and creating a goal of three years for ELL students to exit special instruction). The Coalition also expressed support for Hamer's policy recommendations (including, discontinuing the practice of moving ELLs between bilingual and ESL programs, developing specific interventions for all older ELLs entering at Grade 6 or later, and expanding dual language programs). Lastly, the Coalition endorsed several of the author's recommendations meant to resolve systemic issues not addressed in the *Progress Report*.

On the evening of November 15th, I and other Coalition leaders mobilized more than 60 speakers and an audience of 150 supporters at the "open agenda" portion of a public meeting of the Board of Education. There was a total absence of newspaper coverage of this "people's teach-in." However, board members and the chancellor continued to receive phone calls, e-mail messages, testimonies from local and national experts, and other letters in support of the Coalition's consensus position and in opposition to the English immersion model and the "parental choice" or "opt-in" mechanism favored by the mayor and his allies.

On December19th, Levy released his *Chancellor's report on the education of English language learners* (Levy, 2000). He recommended adding a fourth program model ("Accelerated English Language program") to the three prevalent program models, and asking parents "to make program choices on the basis of written, signed informed consent." In effect, he was proposing to turn the Consent Decree on its head, moving from the court-negotiated "opt-out" mechanism out of bilingual program to an "opt-in" mechanism based on a menu of four choices of equal standing. The $75 million price tag for the implementation of all of Levy's seven proposed policies was immediately shot down by Mayor Giuliani, despite the fact that Levy had accepted most, if not all, of the policy recommendations proposed by the mayor's Task Force.

The *New York Post* ran an editorial lambasting Levy for having "no sense of bilingual ed's utter failure" and for not having "learned from the compelling lessons of California," where, the Post asserted, "Two years later, test scores are up across the board for the former bilingual-ed students" (New York Post, 2000, December 29, p. 32). Former USC researcher, Stephen Krashen, submitted a letter to the editor, rebutting the Post's assertions by citing research analyses of California's test scores (S. Krashen, personal communication, December 30, 2000). But, as in so much of this "perfect storm," he went unpublished and was invisible to the public.

In the end, the chancellor's political compromise between the mayor and Unz's intent to dismantle bilingual education and the bilingual advocates' call for comprehensive reform and significant new resources won the day. After another series of public hearings (113 speakers testified and 200 bilingual supporters attended one such hearing at the Board of Education on January 24, 2001), tabloid importuning, and private arm-twisting, the chancellor's seven policy goals were approved unanimously by the Board of Education on February 27, 2000.

Time will tell what improvements came out of this winter storm of bilingual controversy. Suffice it to say Giuliani only provided $9 million for Saturday and summer English immersion classes. All the other policy initiatives went unfunded; the systemic issues went unaddressed; and everybody ignored the "bilingual issue" until a new mayor was elected in November 2001. Five weeks after his inauguration, Mayor Michael Bloomberg declared his support for "total English immersion." This new "storm" promises to be another truly big one as the new mayor also seeks "total mayoral control" of the school system. But, that's a story for another time!

REFERENCES

ASPIRA of New York, Inc. v. Board of Education, 394 F. Supp. 1161 (S.D.N.Y. 1975).

Holloway, L. (2000, October 17). Immersion promoted as alternative to bilingual instruction. *The New York Times,* pp. A1, A8.

Levy, H. O. (2000, December). *Chancellor's report on the education of English language learners.* New York: New York City Board of Education.

Mastro, R. M. (2000, September 24). How New York can fix bilingual education. *Daily News,* p. 23.

New York City Board of Education. (2000, September). *English language learners (ELL) subcommittee research studies progress report.* New York: Division of Assessment and Accountability.

New York City Board of Education. (2000, October). *Facts and figures 1999–2000: Answers to frequently asked questions about English language learners (ELL) and bilingual/ESL programs.* New York: Office of Bilingual Education.

New York Daily News. (2000, October 24). Straight talk for immigrant kids. *Daily News,* p. 48.

New York Post. (2000, December 29). A school reform that isn't. *New York Post,* p. 23.

Reyes, L. O. (1999, December). *Testimony on bilingual education in New York City: Hearing before the New York State Assembly Standing Committee on Education.* Unpublished manuscript.

Reyes, L. O. (2000, October). *Testimony on bilingual education in New York City at public hearing of the Mayor's Task Force on Bilingual education.* Unpublished manuscript.

Tierney, J. (2000, October 17). The secret to becoming bilingual. *The New York Times,* p. A1.

Tierney, J. (2000, December 19). When crutch for education is an anchor. *The New York Times,* p. A1.

JOURNAL OF LATINOS AND EDUCATION, 2(1), 31–37

Teachers' (re)Constructions of Knowledge: The Other Side of Fieldwork

Xaé Alicia Reyes

Neag School of Education and Puerto Rican and Latino Studies Institute
University of Connecticut, Storrs

Latino students continue to have high dropout rates and are affected by a culture of low expectations and stereotypical notions regarding who they are. Messages conveyed by news reports and media representations continue to misinform mainstream audiences, which include teachers, regarding the cultural context and characteristics of Latinos. More community involvement during field placements, collaborations between academics and host communities, and validation of insider narratives are needed to construct factual knowledge about Latino students in order to better meet their needs.

Key words: Latino/a, students, teacher education, stereotypes, fieldwork, community

The cultural mismatch between teachers and their students (Darder, 1991; Nieto, 1992, 1996) prompts an overreliance on superficial, or sensationalized data as the knowledgebase on students from diverse backgrounds. Oftentimes, teachers have not ventured out of their own experiential and biographical circumstances. Their mobility and interactions with people from socioeconomic, racial, ethnic, cultural, and linguistic backgrounds different from theirs, is often too limited. In my experience with pre-service educators for the last 10 years, I continue to find that they have had little exposure to people different from themselves. Countless autobiographical writings describe the lack of interactions outside of their cultural boundaries. Furthermore, in spite of years of education courses and exposure to theories and research, most choose to teach as they were taught, rather than to follow the

---

Requests for reprints should be sent to Xaé Alicia Reyes, Neag School of Education U-2033, University of Connecticut, Storrs, Storrs, CT 06269. E-mail: xreyes@uconn.edu

more student-centered teaching practices emphasized and encouraged by progressive educators such as Freire (1972). This discussion will focus on how teachers construct knowledge about "others" and how a more contextualized approach to fieldwork may contribute to a more reliable knowledge base. An example of how teachers' have been informing their knowledge about their students came about very recently, when a graduate education student conducted research regarding the increasing number of Latinos in a northeastern school. She asked a teacher how the needs of the diverse students were being met and the teacher responded,

> The minorities run the school and have such a lack of respect for authority and rules. There is no support system for teachers trying to make a difference. [I wonder what kind of difference she is talking about—Interviewer] Even the principal runs scared. Everyone, including the teachers are waiting for the school year to end. Meanwhile the students are learning nothing, including my daughter. Minorities control and are even allowed to sit through class with headphones on. The students are disrespectful to me and when I complain, I get zero results. Administrators just look the other way and do not get involved. I have never considered myself prejudiced but I do now. I call my students "sharks." The educational system stinks! (Teacher interview, April 2002)

Reading this interview, in 2002, one cannot imagine that the impact of *West Side Story* (Wise & Robbins, 1961) is still present in today's environment. Calling the Latinos "sharks," as the Puerto Rican group in the movie were called, and then implying that they inspired fear in teachers and administrators shows the deep roots of bias exposed in her discourse. The graduate student who conducted the interview happened to be aware of the frameworks to make the connections to the media images. Those of us in the interviewee's peer group can certainly remember the success of this Broadway play that is still appealing. However, a larger number of our teacher education students were unable to identify the reference and would thus take the word *sharks* at face value with its negative connotations.

In this article, I move toward the solution to the artificially constructed knowledge about "the other." It is not my intention to analyze the media depictions of Latina/os, but I would like to highlight a more realistic and less known film called *In a Class of His Own* (Munic, 1999), where a Latino custodian, played by Lou Diamond Philips, is the most significant adult to Latina/o students in a high school. The focus of the movie is the fact that he has not completed high school and this information is used to undermine his credibility as an "advisor" and de facto counselor to the students. The real value of this film is the message related to the cultural connections between the custodian and the students. This is significant because it reflects a reality that is quite visible in our Latino communities and which presses me to emphasize the need for connections with *all* participants in the school settings. Cafeteria staff, custodians, security guards, parents, paraprofessionals, and other staff outside of the teachers and administrators are often rendered invisible by academics and their students involved in fieldwork in schools.

FIELD-INTENSIVE TEACHER EDUCATION

Teacher education programs have increased their fieldwork in order to inform teachers about their students and their communities in ways that books and class discussions could never be able to. The need for a more encompassing approach to these experiences is an imperative to making this a meaningful experience that will truly inform practice. If the population of students in our teacher education programs continues to be predominantly White, middle-class females, we are lacking the critical mass to engage in dialogues that will challenge our understandings of "the other." The need to draw knowledge from the fieldwork is abundantly clear, but the real understandings will only occur with the "soaking in" of all possible dimensions of this experience.

The variety of approaches to create the sense of what is "real" in our schools and classrooms varies in intensity from one teacher education program to another. We also find that some programs require field placements at the onset of admission into teacher education while others intensify and begin the exposure the year prior to student teaching. All of these approaches meet with varying levels of success, but most success comes with the individual's commitment to and interest in the community where the field placement occurs. In addition to this, the effectiveness or lack thereof is often related to the modeling of this commitment and of the involvement of the institution and of its faculty members. When is fieldwork meaningful? When do our students really integrate the experiences of working in the field into their conscious understanding of teaching and learning? Does it really happen? How much of the success is proportionate or reflective of the involvement of the faculty in the setting and the positioning with regard to teachers and other community members such as parents and staff at schools? How do these experiences clarify our understandings of the "other"?

There has to be a recognition of one's own baggage in order to explain one's understandings of a situation, in this case of the schooling experiences of others. I try to model the importance of this analysis by sharing my own "discoveries" of significant factors that made a difference in access to education. For example, I was never aware of my status as a first-generation college student and of the implications of that status. I had struggled with my adjustment to college and had observed how easy it was for some of my peers to navigate the system; they knew what courses to take and who the professors were and they understood adding and dropping and appeared to be at home in the setting. I made it through, but it was definitely not seamless. Years later, I was asked to direct a program for first-generation college students (see Martinez, 2003). As I became immersed in the program objectives and the literature, I found myself identifying with the characteristics of the students I was now to serve. Other experiences began to have meaning as well. My bilingualism, which I treasure, had been possible because I was an Army dependent and my parents encouraged fluency in both languages. Although both had only completed high school, they placed high value on correction and proficiency in both languages. Our circulatory migration patterns required entering and exiting schools where the dominant language varied between English and Spanish.

In conducting and reporting fieldwork, I feel it is important to explain how our own backgrounds and experiences interface with those of our host communities. It is important to clarify what aspects of our experiences are similar and those where we have differences. Our readers and listeners need to make sense of this to validate our data and make meaning of them as well. Thus, I appreciate Guadalupe Valdés' (1996) clarifications of her own background in her ethnographic portrait of Mexican immigrant families in *Con respeto,* where she says,

> To a great degree, there was much that I had in common with the mothers who were part of the study .... I had experienced the sadness in leaving Mexico ... I had also raised children in this country ... I was a native speaker of northern Mexican Spanish. (p. 10)

And further, she states,

> In other ways, it was apparent that I was quite different ... My family was and is part of what in the Mexican world is known as *las clases acomodadas* (people of means) ... My father was a cardiologist ... My family then was part of a stable middle class that never left Mexico .... I am the only one who, as an adult, made the decision to live and stay in the United States. (p. 10)

This information is helpful as we analyze the data and it becomes clear to us that what we notice, what we focus on and how we perceive situations might very well be influenced by our own experiences.

In addition to our experiences, we are influenced overtly and subtly by media images and information. The constant reports of failure on standardized tests, high dropout rates, and crime statistics reported by newspapers linger in our subconscious and very few people probe further to understand the bigger picture. Headlines that cloud our views of the "other" need to be addressed in classrooms and this often requires digressions or departures from scripted lesson plans and/or teaching to the test models. One needs to make a habit of addressing current reports that omit facts such as limited resources and their impact on access to adequate legal defense, and limited resources and staffing to meet needs of students in districts where schools have been labeled as "failing" schools. Ultimately these media messages create an atmosphere of hopelessness that impacts teachers, students, and communities. It influences funding and policy decisions as well.

The pervasiveness of reports and media images is frightening because they appear factual, and even instances of ridicule on film seem harmless; yet we are all subjected to their subtle conditioning. In reading Giroux's (1994) *Disturbing Pleasures: Learning Popular Culture*, I was "disturbed" to acknowledge the level of ridicule reflected in Robin Williams apparently harmless poking fun at English language learners in *Good Morning, Vietnam* (Levinson, 1987). Sometime later I witnessed a father walking out of a supermarket with a toddler in his shopping cart making funny noises to emulate the speech of an Asian couple walking by them. The child giggled playfully and I remembered the scene from the movie. Too many of our attitudes toward difference include patterns of ridicule, name-calling, and blatant disrespect. It has only been recently that events such as those of September 11 and Columbine have pointed to the need to contextualize education to include the everyday realities of the world outside of the classroom (Reyes, 2002). Thus, understanding the context of a school includes knowing the neighborhoods and the social dynamics of their residents as well as the power structures that impact policy. This contextualization referred to as "macrocontextualization" (Osborn, 2002) is the real essence of meaningful and potentially transformative fieldwork. In the context of language learning, I consider this interaction with ethnic cultures and languages comparable to migratory experiences.

FIELDWORK IN THE BROADER CONTEXT

Although we have reconfigured many of our teacher education programs to include frequent and varied interactions in classrooms for our students, many important features are missed. When dealing with diversity issues in my courses, I ask my teacher education students how many have attended a "pow-wow" or an ethnic festival and only a handful of students raise their hands. I am taken aback by this lack of basic curiosity or fear of their surroundings. In a region where celebrations of ethnic heritage are a common feature, one could literally participate in a different cultural experience every weekend. Religious diversity is part of the history of this country and protected by the constitution. This does not appear to inspire people to learn about other practices and beliefs. The meaning behind symbols such as a menorrah in the local synagogue and the ritual of making the sign of the cross I observe in the passenger in the car ahead of me as she drives by a Catholic church are inviting to me. They invite me to learn and compare traditions. I see so many opportunities to learn about each other and I am intrigued by the lack of curiosity or interest on the part of my students. Is it perhaps a validation of the series of traits assigned to people from the United States in so many textbooks that look at cultural features of groups and produce lists that outsiders are to go by in order to interact with "Americans"? Included in these lists is the quest for privacy and individual satisfaction that might dictate a need to render what is different as invisible. These very same traits might contribute to viewing inquisitive interest as prying and violating privacy. These issues create gray areas between what is culturally appropriate, and genuine and legitimate interest in others. Drawing boundaries and interpreting areas of privacy can result in justification for distance and disinterest. It is critical to have discussions about these topics in classrooms and communities in order to improve our understandings of each other and to diminish the overreliance on fabricated media images.

A meaningful field experience requires knowledge of the community by the facilitator or teacher educator who oversees this process. It is not enough to assign hours in a field placement and to speak of service learning if one has not gleaned knowledge of the community beforehand or at least alongside our students. In Apple's (2000) discussion of building of community in an academic setting among teacher educators and their students he states, "Community is best developed out of shared experiences" (p. 151). His discussion centers on the building of community in an academic setting and the tensions related to political views, differences among disciplines, issues of power, and oppression in graduate programs and the ultimate underlying fact that caring communities "are grounded in people's lives. Both people and the lives can and do change" (p. 152). While one could argue that the community in academia is a separate issue, the truth is that, if academia is not in touch with the community and working within its context, it is a location or site of little relevance in the development of better societies. Hence, it is important to build community within academia and include the greater community in a joint construction of meaning.

Finally, these dialogues will inform our knowledge of "the other" and allow us to separate fact from fiction. These conversations can only take place if we are part of the fabric of those communities and if we converge in the sites that are important for authentic dialogues in the community. In *Teachers and Texts*, Apple (1988) says that critical scholarship in education is

> not merely a commodity to be "bought" and "sold" in the academic marketplace … Those who engage in critical scholarship in education should have constant and close ties to the real world of teachers, students, and parents … and they need to be closely connected to feminist groups, people of color, and those teachers and curriculum workers who are now struggling for gains that have been made in democratizing education and to make certain that our schools and the curricular and teaching practices within them are responsive in race, gender, and class terms. (pp. 203–204)

Furthermore, our interactions with the "other" and in communities need to be framed in an atmosphere of reciprocity where we learn from each other and view each other as contributors. Our dialogues need to be positioned evenly. We cannot allow ourselves and our students to assume hegemonic stances, whereby we view the "others" as deficient and ourselves as redeemers.

REFERENCES

Apple, M. (1988). *Teachers and texts: A political economy of class and gender relations in education.* Boston: Routledge.

Apple, M. (2000). *Official Knowledge: democratic education in a conservative age.* New York: Routledge.

Darder, A. (1991). *Culture and power in the classroom: a critical foundation for bilingual education.* New York: Bergin and Garvey.

Freire, P. (1972). *Pedagogía del oprimido.* Ciudad de México, México: SigloVeintiuno Editores.

Giroux, H. (1994). *Disturbing pleasures: learning popular culture.* New York: Routledge.

Levinson, B. (Director). (1987). *Good morning, Vietnam* [Motion Picture]. United States: Touchstone Pictures.

Martinez, M. (2003). Missing in action: Reconstructing hope and possiblity among Latino students placed at risk. *Journal of Latinos and Education, 2,* 13–21.

Munic, R. (Director). (1999). *In a class of his own* [Motion Picture]. ShowTime Network, Inc.

Nieto, S. (1996). *Affirming diversity: the sociopolitical context of multicultural education* (2nd ed.). White Plains, NY: Longman.

Osborn, T. (2000). *Critical reflection and the foreign language classroom.* Wesport, CT: Bergin and Garvey.

Reyes, X. A. (2002). Authentic migratory experiences for language learners: Macrocontextualization as critical pedagogy. In T. A. Osborn (Ed.), *The future of foreign language education in the United States.* Wesport, CT: Greenwood.

Valdés, G. (1996). *Con respeto, bridging the distances between culturally diverse families and schools: and ethnographic portrait.* New York: Teachers College Press.

Wise, R. (Director), & Robbins, J. (Director). (1961). *West side story* [Motion Picture]. United States: United Artists.

JOURNAL OF LATINOS AND EDUCATION, 2(1), 39–46

When Education, Media, and Technology Converge, What Do Latino/a Students Gain?

Dolores Valencia Tanno

Greenspun School of Communication
University of Nevada, Las Vegas

The convergence of technology, media, and education has the potential to impact the successes and failures of Latino/a students in higher education. Research suggests success for these students is closely linked with the amount of face-to-face, interpersonal relationships they experience with faculty and staff. The convergence, however, promises less rather than more of this type of interaction. More research is required on the successes, failures, and worldviews of Latino/a students in higher education in order to reverse the current college dropout trend.

Key words: Latino/a, technology, technological access, worldview, mediated education, convergence

The conditions of production and consumption of education and its technologies, while they may have undergone subtle shifts, have not … significantly altered the unequal power relations between the educational producers and the "peripheral" consumers of education. (Ashcroft, Griffiths, & Tiffin, 1995, p. 425)

Fact: Education, media, and technology are interdependent. Fact: There are low percentages of Latino/as pursuing higher education and large percentages of Latino/as dropping out of high school and college. Fact: The generation of students currently in institutions of higher education seem to share a world-view that impacts how they perceive what education is and what it is for.

Requests for reprints should be sent to Dolores Valencia Tanno, Greenspun School of Communication, University of Nevada Las Vegas, Las Vegas, NV 89154–5007. E-mail: dtanno@ccmail.nevada.edu

The first part of this article provides a brief review of research supporting these facts. The second part focuses on the convergence of these facts and the impact of this convergence on research about Latino/a students in higher education. Throughout, I share caveats that underscore the need for more research on Latino/a students.

PART I

Technology

It is difficult to conceive, in current reality, an educational system that is not at least partially reliant on teaching technology (instructional software, multimedia materials, distance learning) as the "answer" to various problems. These problems range from how to help students become more technologically sophisticated to how to reach students in distant places to how to appeal to students' learning processes. We are looking for ways to mediate information for students whose lives have been shaped in various degrees by media and technology and whose informational habits seem intimately tied to these.

In *Issues in Web-Based Pedagogy: A Critical Primer*, Cole (2000) provides some reasons for why we view technology as the panacea for education. We tend to view technology as liberating and egalitarian, Cole argues, because we believe it

- Frees us from the normal educational constraints (schedules imposed by others, such as class days and times).
- Allows for the widespread delivery of information (distance learning).
- Allows greater as well as equal accessibility between student and teacher. (Cole, 2000, p. ix)

But Cole (2000) also cautions that teaching technology is more time-consuming for both student and teacher. More important, in the context of Latino/a students in higher education, technology only offers an illusion of egalitarianism. We tend to think of technology as propelling us forward, but Cole argues technology may be pushing us backward because technology splits the mind and the body. This mind–body split results in the disconnect of experience from cognition and "learning by thinking" (p. xi) from "learning by doing" (p. x).

Robinson (2000) argues that teaching technology, with all its otherwise good qualities, also has what she perceives to be a negative quality. Students learn and produce in a "sterile place, not a communal place" (p. 120). She goes on to say, "it is like having a class where the students are seated outside the door in cubicles separating them from interaction. They never enter the classroom, but reside outside" (p. 120). Paris (2000) also implicates technology, to some degree, for the change in educational perspective that now thinks of customers and name-brand schools and for-profit institutions (pp. 102–103).

That technology is a fixture in educational institutions is a given; that it is equally "fixed" is not. In a study that challenges the "appropriate" use of technology in teaching, Kilker (2000) compares a commuter school with an ivy league school in terms of availability of technology, access to technology, and uses of technology. His comparisons are astonishing even to those of us who have known it all along

- In the commuter institution students had significantly less computer experience; use of computer technology was minimal and optional; students had to locate/use computers on their own; and even technology-based courses were taught in traditional non-wired classrooms.
- In the ivy league institution students had significantly more computer experience; use of computer technology was intensive and required; and students had one computer per student in a wired classroom.

Finally Fitzgerald (1995), in an article titled "Cyberspace Sin Fronteras," argues that "cyberspace is taking on a Spanish accent" (p. 64) in the publishing context as the internet "builds communities across borders" (p. 64) among Latino/a journalists. The emphasis on online publishing has led to greater and greater access to technology and thus to greater and greater technological skills among journalists. If similar egalitarian access and technological proficiency were present in our colleges and universities for Latino/a students we could describe technology in higher education as "cyberspace sin fronteras" (without borders); unfortunately, at the present time, it is more realistic to describe it as cyberspace con fronteras (with borders).

Latino/as in Higher Education

I do not mean to dwell on the more difficult and negative implications of educational technology but I do so for one very simple reason: The rate of success (or lack thereof) of Latino/as in higher education is woefully small. We are all aware of the statistics (Hispanic Association of Colleges and Universities [HACU]: Facts on Hispanic Higher Education, 2001):

- Hispanics account for 11.4% of the population.
- One of every four persons living in poverty in the United States is of Hispanic origin.
- 1.36 million Hispanics are enrolled in higher education in the United States.
- 71.2% of all Hispanics have never attended college and 13.3% have attended "some" college.

- Hispanics constituted 6.9% of associate degrees; 5.0% of bachelor's degrees; 3.6% of master's degrees; 4.5% of first-professional degrees; and 2.2% of all doctorate degrees awarded.
- Nearly 40% of Hispanic students who drop out do so before eighth grade.
- By 1998, for persons 25 years old and over, only 11% of Hispanics had completed a college education.

From my specific perspective as a resident, Nevada is a state whose population is 26% Latino/a; the University of Nevada, Las Vegas, has an enrollment of 7% Latino/as and, like many other universities, a poor record of retaining these students through graduation.

There is another fact to consider: Latino/as that attend college often do so in commuter-type institutions where teaching technology is not always adequate nor equitably accessible to all students, as Kilker's study demonstrates.

Let me shift now to studies that focus on what it is that makes Latino/as enroll, achieve, and get a degree. Anaya and Cole (2001) explore the influence of student–faculty interaction on GPA; Hernández (2000) studies what it is that helps Latino/as stay in college. It is important to underscore the significant lack of studies on Latino/a students in higher education; Anaya and Cole's and Hernández's studies represent two of the most recent.

The methodologies of these two studies are different. Anaya and Cole's (2001) study is a straight-forward quantitative study using a 191-item survey and a dependent variable of academic achievement using a sample of 836 undergraduate Latino/a students in 30 research and doctoral-granting institutions. Hernández's (2000) study is a qualitative analysis based on personal experiences and environmental factors of 10 Latino/a students (5 male, 5 female). What is interesting is that, from different beginning points and with different methodologies, these studies reach the same conclusion. University success for Latino/a students is correlated with personal, consistent, face-to-face interaction with faculty, staff, and students in general, and other Latino/a students in particular. Anaya and Cole (2001) emphasize that the interaction involves academic as well as general and personal matters and that it is important to foster this interaction both "in and beyond the classroom" (p. 12). Hernández points out that perhaps the single most influential factor affecting retention is to have faculty and staff validate the students' desires to succeed, especially those who are unfamiliar with the college environment and who are first-generation college attendees.

Thus we have opposing forces at work. First, we have studies suggesting technology and education are becoming increasingly and inextricably intertwined. This impacts our conceptions of pedagogy—distance learning, web-based learning, and so forth—that, if not completely foregoing face-to-face interaction, nevertheless potentially operate on less-than an interpersonal-relationship level.

Second, we have the studies of Latino/as in higher education suggesting a major reason Latino/as get though the college years successfully is because of the personal, face-to-face relationships they forge with other students and especially with faculty and staff.

Just at the time when more Latino/a students are attending college, the conditions of education are changing. Success at the university is, at least in part, dependent on such things as the student's technological sophistication, one-to-one computer/student access in classrooms, and the ability of the student to succeed academically without expecting or relying on personal, face-to-face interaction and support. Implied in all of this is that all students have equal as well as consistent access to technology, and all students work equally well with less rather than more face-to-face interaction.

Generational Worldviews

It is not just the conditions of education that are changing; it is also the worldviews and values of those who seek higher education. I want to share with you some of the research findings in this area, but I do so with a significant caveat: most of these studies do not indicate the ethnic/racial backgrounds of the participants in the surveys/interviews. It seems to me probable that a breakdown of these might indicate differences in goals and values among students of different ethnic/racial backgrounds, especially if they represent—as many Latino/a students do—the first generation of their families to pursue higher education.

Easterlin and Crimmins's (1991) study is based on two annual national surveys, one of college freshmen (Cooperative Institutional Research Program) and the other of high school seniors (University of Michigan Survey Research Center). Easterlin and Crimmins conclude that, since the 1970s, a shift has occurred in the value orientations of American youth. This shift has resulted in "a substantial increase in private materialism as a life goal," "a modest turning away from the public interest," and "a sharp decline in emphasis on personal self-fulfillment" (p. 529). Together, these have resulted in trends that show "an increase in importance of [jobs] related to money and status and decreased importance of those related to public interest and personal fulfillment" (p. 529). I must interject a note here. Being involved with Latino/a students in higher education over the course of 15 years, it has been my observation that Latino/a students tend to be public-interest minded. They often choose assignment foci and/or majors with the idea that they want to be prepared "to give back to the community." The caveat, again, is that research is necessary to determine whether most, some, or only a few Latino/a students fit this description. Perhaps what is most revealing in this study is the cause to which Easterlin and Crimmins attribute this shift: it is us, the adults that surround students—parents, teachers, public figures, and so forth—who have, it seems, emphasized private materialism to the near-exclusion of public interest and self-fulfillment. Being reflected back to us, in varying degrees, is our own preoc- cupation with success and status.

But how reflective of these conclusions are first-generation Latino/a students, or African American students or Pacific-Rim students or Native American stu- dents? All together these students certainly represent a small percentage of the totality of college freshmen students providing the data on which Easterlin and Crimmins's (1991) study was based. I say "certainly" because, in sum, these stu- dents constitute a small number of students in higher education across the na- tion.

In another study, Levine and Cureton (1998) describe the current generation of students as the "transitional generation." They argue that, like history, student bodies evolve cyclically. They describe these cycles as (a) "periods of commu- nity ascendency" (p. 146), when students are awake to change and reform and are more outward-looking and future-oriented, and (b) "periods of individual ascendency," when, feeling weary and tired, they seek rest, turn their focus in- ward, and become more rooted in getting than giving (p. 146). Levine and Cureton advance the idea that today's generation of students is in a transition state between these two cycles: neither awake nor resting, neither outward nor inward-focused. This transitional generation is a blend of characteristics that ap- pear to be forces in opposition, but they also appear to be facts of contemporary life for students. For example, students are simultaneously demanding change and desperately committed to preserving the American dream; sexually active but socially isolated; diverse and divided but optimistic about their collective fu- ture; and weak in basic skills, frightened and tired, but nevertheless committed to doing well and doing good (pp. 156–157).

Other studies corroborate many of these characteristics and/or offer others. Newton (2000), for example, conducted a study of approximately 200 students in a midwestern university. Based on the data gathered through "personal vignettes and commentary" (p. 9), Newton argues that today's students tend to have greater experience in "grown-up activity" (p. 9). They know more and can access greater amounts of knowledge but are less able to critically assess information because they have less "discipline and focus" (p. 9). Further, they experience "increasingly high levels of stress and anxiety" (p. 10). Newton's analysis of the data leads him to also suggest female students express "twice as much stress as their male coun- terparts" (p. 10). He attributes these and other characteristics to "large-scale sys- temic change" (p. 12) resulting in feelings of alienation and instability in students. Such feelings prompt students to seek a degree of coherence in their environment. In seeking coherence, students become skill-focused, pragmatic and status- and money-oriented. These attributes are perceived by students as the means to finding an organizing structure for finding a sense of meaningfulness in their chaotic envi- ronment.

PART II

The caveats cited throughout suggest the insufficiency of the research available about Latino/a students in higher education. How many of the characteristics attributed to today's college students also describe Latino/a students or students of other minority groups? How many of these characteristics do not? What does all this mean for Latino/a students in higher education? Fundamentally, I think, it means that unless we are able to fully understand how all of these elements converge and affect the success rate of Latino/a students in our colleges and universities, we cannot find ways to help them through the process. There are many research foci that would help us gain this understanding, but I suggest only five here.

First, how does the convergence of technology and higher education impact Latino/as in higher education? What exactly is the degree and consistency of accessibility to technology that Latino/a students experience in higher education? How technologically sophisticated are Latino/a students? This information will help us better understand and better determine what we can do to support, educate, and matriculate Latino/a students in an educational environment that is bound to get more rather than less dependent on technology.

Second, what does it mean that, in many cases, Latinos in higher education are first-generation attendees? How does this fact impact issues of technological access and sophistication? In what ways might this portend a difference in how Latino/a students perceive what education is and what education is for?

Third, should we assume all college students are the products of mediated education? Channel One is used in many elementary classrooms; middle schools work to equip classrooms with technology; high schools are increasingly using web-based pedagogy. Colleges and universities are increasingly relying on distance education. But at all of these levels, are these equally accessible and equally distributed among schools and among students? If not, as Kilker's study demonstrates, what does this mean for those students who do not have the benefit of technological sophistication gained from elementary school on? The possibility of yet another type of marginalization looms large.

Fourth, there is sufficient research literature to suggest that technology may not be neutral. Bowers (1988) argued technology was not "gender-neutral" (p. 91) because women interacted differently with technology from men. He further argued that "in the case of women, this involves reconciling their own sense of integrity about what is intellectually and morally important with the conceptual and value-laden agenda that males have designed into the computer" (p. 92). I bring this up, whether we agree this is so or not, because it does open to debate the question of neutral technology and because it makes me wonder: If technology is not gender-neutral, could it be that it is also not ethnic- or race-neutral?

Fifth and finally, why do Latino/a students drop out of education? There are studies that provide some understanding about why this is so, but there is a real dearth of studies that explore the successes of our Latino/a students in higher education. We need to understand both the successes and the failures if we are to provide the necessary support for getting to and through college.

I am fully aware that I pose many more questions than I have answers. I do this because I am convinced we need to know more and do more about on the impact of mediated education on Latino/a students whose college attendance rates are too low and whose drop-out rates are too high. The more we know, the greater the possibility that we can reverse these trends.

REFERENCES

Anaya, G., & Cole, D. G. (2001). Latina/o student achievement: Exploring the influence of student-faculty interactions on college grades. *Journal of College Student Development*, *42*, 3–14.

Ashcroft, B., Griffiths, G., & Tiffin, H. (1995). Introduction to part XIII: Education. In B. Ashcroft, G. Griffiths, & H. Tiffin (Eds.), *The postcolonial studies reader* (pp. 425–427). New York: Routledge.

Bowers, C. A. (1988). *The cultural dimensions of educational computing: Understanding the non-neutrality of technology*. New York: Teachers Press.

Cole, R. A. (Ed.). (2000). *Issues in web-based pedagogy: A critical primer*. Westport, CT: Greenwood.

Easterlin, R. A., & Crimmins, E. M. (1991). Private materialism, personal self-fulfillment, family life, and public interest: The nature, effects and causes of recent changes in the values of American youth. *Public Opinion Quarterly*, *55*, 499–533.

Fitzgerald, M. (1995). Cyberspace sin fronteras. *The Fourth Estate*, *28*, 64.

Hispanic Association of Colleges and Universities (HACU): Facts on Hispanic higher education. (2001). Retrieved March 14, 2001, from http://www.hacu.com/publications/facts.htm

Hernández, J. C. (2000). Understanding the retention of Latino college students. *Journal of College Student Development*, *41*, 575–588.

Kilker, J. (2000). When and where appropriate: Lessons from "foreign" contexts for the pedagogical use of web-based technologies in the United States. In R. A. Cole (Ed.), *Issues in web-based pedagogy: A critical primer* (pp. 65–79). Westport, CT: Greenwood.

Levine, A., & Cureton, J. S. (1998). *When hope and fear collide: A portrait of today's college student*. San Francisco: Jossey-Bass.

Newton, F. B. (2000, November/December). The new student. *About Campus*, *5*, 8–15.

Paris, D. C. (2000). Is there a professor in this class? In R. A. Cole (Ed.), *Issues in web-based pedagogy: A critical primer* (pp. 95–110). Westport, CT: Greenwood.

Robinson, P. (2000). Where is everybody? In R. A. Cole (Ed.), *Issues in web-based pedagogy: A critical primer* (pp. 11–123). Westport, CT: Greenwood.

JOURNAL OF LATINOS AND EDUCATION, 2(1), 47–57

The Latin Grammys and the ALMAs: Awards Programs, Cultural Epideictic, and Intercultural Pedagogy

Alberto González and Amy N. Heuman

Bowling Green State University

This article is not about Latino educators, nor is it about Latinos-as-students in educational settings. Our concern is Latino peoples and cultures as a curricular object—*Latino/as as course content*. This article examines 2 media texts, the Latin Grammy Awards and the ALMA Awards. We argue that the awards programs, and their didactic qualities, arise from and are a reaction to a profound social realization of the Latino presence. We begin by outlining our critical reformulation of epideictic rhetoric. Second, we provide background on the 2 programs and interpret their import as epideictic discourse. Finally, we offer some preliminary guides as instructional materials on Latino cultures.

The only thing I want to teach is what I want to learn. (Gloria Anzaldúa, 2000, p. 68)

This article is not about Latino educators, nor is it about Latinos-as-students in educational settings. Our concern is Latino peoples and cultures as a curricular object—*Latino/as as course content*. The focus of our critique is, as Anzaldúa (2000) intimates in the previous quotation, an occurrence of Latinos and Latinas teaching what they want to learn about themselves as a people. They teach on a stage rather than a classroom. Yet the honoring of their work in the entertainment industry is available as media texts that can be used as an instructional tool in the intercultural communication course. Our critical method is a rhetorical examination of two media texts, the Latino Grammys and the ALMA (American Latino Media Arts) Awards.

Requests for reprints should be sent to Alberto González, Bowling Green State University, 305 McFall Center, Bowling Green, OH 43403. E-mail: Agonzal@bgnet.bgsu.edu

Our goal in engaging in cultural criticism is to illustrate and understand how an ethnic identity comes to life through its symbolic expressions, or more broadly, how it lives through the negotiation of its symbols. In our view, nowhere in the current social scene do we see meanings so intensely created, enacted, and contested, than among Latinos and Latinas generally, and in Latino/a media texts specifically. The intensity of play surrounding meanings in Latino cultures has rich implications for educators who rightly choose to expand student awareness and knowledge about Latino/as.

This article examines two media texts, the Latin Grammy Awards and the ALMA Awards. We argue that the awards programs, and their didactic qualities, arise from and are a reaction to a profound social realization of the Latino presence. The first section of this article outlines our critical reformulation of epideictic rhetoric. The second section provides background on the two programs and interprets their import as epideictic discourse. The final section provides some preliminary guides for the inclusion of awards shows as instructional materials on Latino cultures.

EPIDEICTIC RHETORIC AT THE LATINO GRAMMYS AND THE ALMAS

In the *Rhetoric*, Aristotle (1932) describes three kinds of discourse—deliberative, forensic, and epideictic. Deliberative rhetoric considers the pros and cons of particular policy options and is future oriented. Forensic rhetoric weighs the guilt or innocence of an individual and concerns past events. Epideictic rhetoric directs praise or blame to an individual or condition and is very much set in the present. Epideictic rhetoric is rooted in ceremony and ritual and is relevant to cultural criticism because this oratory most closely relies upon the common knowledge and values held between speaker and audience.

According to Sheard (1996), epideictic "initially meant simply 'lecture' and denoted discourse appropriate within pedagogical or ritual contexts" (p. 766). We continue the association of epideictic with pedagogy. But because speeches of praise or blame focused so centrally on existing values, epideictic rhetoric became associated with a kind of speechmaking "whose principle of operation is amplification" (Poulakos, 1987, p. 324). Music award ceremonies amplify the talents and accomplishments of award recipients. At the Latino Grammy and ALMA awards not only are the performers praised, ethnic identity is amplified as well.

Aristotle viewed rhetoric primarily as a tool for persuasion, whereas we view rhetoric from a perspective that accommodates differences and fragmentation (McKerrow, 1989), as well as the possibility of *communitas* (Turner, 1982). For us, rhetorical communication is the symbolic attempt to facilitate any number of surface goals—adaptation, negotiation, mediation, participation—with the deeper goal of renewing, (re)creating, opposing, or preserving the "sacred centers" of the culture: identity, community, motive, power, and value. Hence, the Latino Grammys and the ALMAs are able to achieve at least three important rhetorical goals—participate in, or perform, Latino identity to preserve it; mediate Latino identities to the non-Latino audiences; and call into question mainstream media practices that exclude Latinos and perpetuate negative stereotypes about Latinos. Simultaneously, the award programs create teaching materials by which educators can present Latino cultural sensibilities in the classroom.

Finally, we view education as a display of epideictic rhetoric. Giroux (1992) observes that "the sphere of higher education represents an important public culture that cultivates and produces stories of how to live ethically and politically; its institutions reproduce selected values" (p. 91). These "stories" are celebrations (or amplifications) not only of canonical endurance but of cultural emphasis. By what gets included and excluded, education symbolically directs praise to particular methods of discovery and analysis (and their products) and blame to others.

LATIN GRAMMYS AND THE ALMAS: OPPORTUNITY AND DISCORD

At the 42nd Annual Grammy Awards in February 2000, actor Jimmy Smits announced that the first-ever Latino Grammy Awards would be televised by CBS in September. Under the auspices of the National Academy of Recording Arts and Sciences, Inc., the Latino Grammys would include 40 award categories that would both parallel and depart from the familiar Grammy awards.

On one level, the Latin Grammys display many similarities to the traditional Grammy Awards. The basic structure is maintained. Participation is restricted to Latin Academy members. Hosts facilitate introductions of presenters and supply transitional commentary before and after commercial breaks. The hosts provide comic relief. In the case of the Latin Grammys, Jimmy Smits, Andy Garcia, and Gloria Estefan engage in typical entertainment industry hyperbole ("music will always unite us," says Jennifer Lopez), frequently used the word *hot*, and traded sexually suggestive comments. Grammy winners had one minute to thank their God, their fans, family, and management firms. Those that attempted to speak longer, like Celia Cruz and Shakira, were musically interrupted.

But on another level, resistance and disjuncture remain possible. José Limón (1998) often isolates collisions between hegemonic norms and artistic expression. As he articulates an emerging postmodernity in South Texas through an interpretation of the late Tejana singer, Selena, he states,

> Conjunto has been celebrated for its "resistive" stance against Anglo America and what has been seen as a "colluding" Mexican middle class, and Selena's performance

of it always contained a gender contradiction, since this musical form traditionally features (almost exclusively) men as performers, male-centered lyrics, and male-dominated dancing. (p. 179)

If Selena's performances of Tejano music contain gender contradictions, then the Latin Grammys and the ALMAs contain ethnic contradictions. Early in the Latin Grammys, the three hosts are introduced, and while Smits and Estefan are clearly exuberant, Garcia remarks that, at CBS, Latinos were only known as "You gave the 'Survivor' timeslot to who?" In that moment, Garcia emphasizes the rarity of the show and their roles as hosts.

The Latin Grammy premiere draws 7.5 million viewers (compared to 28 million viewers for the Grammy Awards broadcast in February), and ranks 9th of 11 shows rated in that timeslot. It is the highest rated show for that evening among viewers 18 to 34, and the show draws strong audiences in Miami, San Antonio, and Los Angeles (Ocaña, 2000, p. 16). Further, it draws over three times as many viewers as the leading Spanish-language awards program, Univision's "*Premio lo Nuestro*" ("Battlin' Latin Music Awards").

Several months after Smits's announcement at the Grammys, in April, the ALMA awards show is recorded. The ALMA Awards is broadcast on June 17, 2000. ALMA was formed by the National Council of La Raza (NCLR) to recognize Latinos in English-language television and film (NCLR, 2000). The ALMA Awards (formerly called the Bravo Awards) were first broadcast on ABC in 1998.

The social significance of these awards programs is not lost on industry observers and content producers. Raul Yzaguirre, 1998 president of the NCLR, states that the ALMA Award program "is not just for Hispanics. We're saying, 'This is who we are as a people,' and it behooves Joe Average to know the Hispanic community, because we're going to be your neighbor, your employee, your customer" (Doss, 1998, p. F47). The *Daily News* calls the Latin Grammys "groundbreaking" and congratulates CBS for airing the program live and including commercials that are completely in Spanish (Kissell, 2000). *Billboard* notes that, even though the Latin Grammys "fell short on several counts," the show is an experiment that "had interesting flares of diversity" (Cobo, 2000, p. 55).

These programs, however, are not without critics. For example, even as the Latin Grammy show is formally announced, some artists voice a fear of segregation within the media arts industry (Valdes-Rodriguez, 1999). It does not go unnoticed that when Jimmy Smits announced at the "regular" Grammy Awards that the Latin Grammys would occur, this was part of an introduction to the Latin segment of the show, a segment in which two of its performers, Marc Anthony and Ricky Martin, were nominated in mainstream pop categories, not Latin categories.

Many oppose the pop-dominated performances. Delgado (2000) comments that the song selection for pop diva Christina Aguilera is inappropriate for the show. She writes that, "The imposition of that style on Latin standards is a travesty" (p. 2). Carlos Bermudez, a producer for Telemundo, complains that the ALMAs recognize work only in English-language media (Beltran, 2000). Further, some critics observe that the paucity of Latino performers makes for repeat and predictable winners, which makes for uninteresting viewing. One such critic, Bianco (1999), in *USA Today*, states, "The ALMA Awards plays more like an unintended exposé of TV's shameful treatment of Hispanic actors and audiences" (p. 12D).

A major conflict occurs when Mexican artists associated with Fonovisa boycott the Latin Grammys. They claim that the Grammys fail to recognize Mexican styles both in nominations and in invitations to perform at the ceremony. Though Fonovisa garnered three Grammy wins, the awards were refused (Snow, 2000; Werner, 2000).

Others think that the Latin Grammys are a vehicle to promote Latin music empresario Emilio Estefan, Jr. Gilbert Moreno, general manager of Fonovisa, states that the Latin Grammys "is a party between Emilio Estefan and Sony ... The Latin Grammys definitely don't represent Latin artists at all" (Valdes-Rodriguez, 2000, p. F3). Estefan was nominated for six awards. Controversy surrounds a $25,000-a-table fund-raiser held by C. Michael Greene, then head of the National Academy of Arts and Sciences, when donors discovered that funds are not tax-deductible and that the Academy does not support charitable causes (Associated Press, 2000). The "Person of the Year" honoree at the fund-raiser was Emilio Estefan (Philips, 2000).

It is clear that the Latin Grammys and the ALMAs are an important development in the entertainment industry. Set against the backdrop of ongoing accusations against the major television networks that they mis- and underrepresent Latino/as, the phenomenal successes of several Latino and Latina performers, and the 2000 U.S. Census, these award shows were poised to create awareness and change perceptions in the ways Latinos and their allies had long anticipated.

EPIDEICTIC DISCOURSES AT THE LATIN GRAMMYS AND THE ALMAS

The two programs make possible the expressions of nostalgia, nationalistic pride, and affirmations of ethnic identity. For example, Celia Cruz thanks the late Tito Puente and others as she accepts her award and invokes a magical and inspired Havana. After receiving an award, Juan Luis Guerra acknowledges his native Dominican Republic. Shakira acknowledges that Columbia is racked by unrest. She states, "I dedicate this award to that country that is going through difficult times right now, but that never, never forgets how to smile. *Para ti, Colombia!*"

Two major discourses emerge that compose the epideictic rhetoric at the Latin Grammys and the ALMAs: the discourse of unity and the discourse of difference.

Discourse of Unity

Early in the ALMAs, Jennifer Lopez states, "The Latino culture has always been here. Our culture is not a fad. We have always been here and we will always be here." In one respect this statement reveals a unified presence or coming together of Latinos while also serving as a reference to the underrepresentation of Latino/as within the media and U.S. culture. This performative moment reminds us of the historical context that surrounds the emergence of Latino award shows on prime time television.

Similarly, early in the Latin Grammys, Antonio Banderas lists many Central and South American countries represented by the evening's nominees. They are, he says, "As Americans would say, 'Latinos.'" The Latinos, he continues, "Are all joined by a common passion—sex." He quickly corrects himself, "Music! Music!" It is the sound, he concludes, "That celebrates what it means to be Latino."

Whether it is Reba McEntire and Jon Secada singing Anne Murray's hit song, "We're all Alone" or Edward James Olmos calling for unity among all people, the 2000 ALMA Awards serves as a performative stage for a discourse of unity. As Reba sings in English and Secada sings in Spanish the coming together of Anglo and Latino cultures is a symbolic blending aimed at unity not only among Latino cultures but also among non-Latino and Latino cultures. This point is made clear as Edward James Olmos says, "There's only one race and that's the human race. The rest is culture."

Actress Denise Richards also engages in discourse that aims to unify yet also magnifies the differences among cultural groups. She says, "The millenium was known for many things. Most significantly for turning a vastly diverse planet into a thriving global village." She goes on to note key roles and diverse occupations that Latino actors have played. Then, she encourages us to come together by saying, "The members [Latino actors] gave us much more than a memorable performance. They point us to a future where we embrace our differences as much as the similarities." Statements such as this, in our view, appear to be culturally sensitive on the surface yet this view tends to gloss over the differences rather than "embrace" them. In this sense, this discourse suggests a particular kind of unity based upon mainstream standards of blending together as one world.

In contrast, talk show host Cristina calls for Latinos to come together as one people for political activism. As Smits quotes her, "We are a diverse culture with great pride in our respective countries of origin. But it will be our ability to unite through common ground issues like education, health, and immigration that will strengthen our position as members of mainstream America. It can happen, it must happen." Both Richards and Cristina invoke visions of unity even as they locate unifying motives in social unity and political unity, respectively.

Discourse of Difference

The discourse of difference operates on two levels. Latinos magnify differences among Latinos and differences from non-Latinos. For example, Jimmy Smits and Gloria Estefan describe the differences between the Latin Grammys and the "February" Grammys. "At the Latin Grammys, you see Christina Aguilera's belly button," says Estefan. "At the February Grammys, you see Luciano Pavorati's belly button," responds Smits. "At the Latin Grammys, you have the best congas money can buy," continues Estefan. "At the February Grammys," says Smits, "you have Britney Spears." The differences between the Spanish and English speaking communities are further emphasized when Smits renames the CBS network, "*Con Bilingual Savor.*"

At the same time, differences among Latinos are emphasized. Smits references the "spectrum of Latin artists from around the world." Before several of the categories are announced, the celebrity performers list the countries represented by the nominees.

Hector Elizondo, of the television series *Chicago Hope*, is quite clear in highlighting how he sees his Latino heritage as being "different." He states, "I am a Latin from Manhattan. A *Nuyorican.*" This playful expression serves as an introduction to his acceptance speech in which he foregrounds the importance of cultural values. He mentions that he learned these values in his home, in his neighborhood, and he thanks his culture for instilling these values in him. He notes that these three—culture, neighborhood, and family—have all informed the values that he holds close. About this he says, "Life is not fair, don't be a victim, whatever happens success is really measured by your capacity to love, if you don't have that you don't have anything, be useful and give back, and no matter what happens have good posture." In this moment, he affirms his identity as a Nuyorican and amplifies the distinctiveness of this identity.

In this same way, Laura Cerón of the television series *ER*, highlights the difference between Latinos and non-Latinos by amplifying the strong bond she has with her family. In one way this is stereotypic, yet she communicates this with sincerity and appreciation. She thanks her father, mother, brothers, and sisters—"David, Rosa, Victor, Gabi, and Marina"—and then all of her nieces and nephews by name. As she thanks each family member by name the crowd laughs in recognition of offering gratitude to la familia as they relate to her desire to do so. She also thanks and makes mention of her neighborhood and home town of Elgin, Illinois. Both acknowledgments point to her unique experiences yet connected experiences as a Latina woman, while Christina Aguilera's acceptance speech, on the other hand, does not have any culturally specific moments of recognition.

Moreover, Laura Cerón offers up a critique of the industry (as do many actors) as she thanks the NCLR. She quips about the industry's lack of Latino/a representation by saying, "Even if they run out of people to nominate" (referring to NCLR). She then quickly notes that that will change as long as we (Latino/a actors) keep working.

A similar critique pointing to difference can be found in the opening skit of the ALMA awards. Paul Rodriguez and another man, referred to as a "Puerto Rican boy from the Bronx," opened the 2000 ALMA Awards with a *Fantasy Island* skit. Rodriquez is Mr. Roark and the other guy is Tattoo. At one point, Rodriguez says that he feels like he is in a "fantasy world" and Tattoo responds by saying that this is the real world. Rodriguez banters back by saying that it feels like a fantasy world because Latinos are on prime time television. This is clearly a critique of the industry's lack of representation when it comes to Latinos in the media.

IMPLICATIONS FOR INTERCULTURAL PEDAGOGY

According to Clark (1996), critical rhetoric is located in "some current, local contingency" (p. 111). The course on Intercultural Communication (IC) is our current, local contingency. In this section, we share some precautions and opportunities for the use of Latino awards programs as a teaching tool in the IC course.

While course objectives vary, the goals of the IC course typically are to apply communication theories to understanding intercultural interaction and enhance skills for communicating in intercultural contexts. Topics in the course usually include: language differences, nonverbal differences, ethics for IC, intercultural conflict, dealing with culture shock, meaning, worldview, and so forth. Course activities usually include role-playing, listening to guest speakers, presenting on cultures other than one's own, and watching videos.

Though the course has fairly identifiable goals and content, the delivery of this content varies widely. There is no orthodoxy for the IC course. Many of us who teach IC courses reflect on a variety of issues: What elements in our own experiences shape how we present the cultural Other? What authors are "credible" interpreters of culture? How do we counter the (often unexpressed) goal of most of our students, namely, to gain intercultural knowledge for economic gain? (We often call this the, "How can I understand you so that I can sell to you" motive.) What do we really want our students to do after having taken the IC course?

As a pedagogical tool, the award shows provide occasions for us to think beyond stereotypes or expedient constructions of Latino/as. Since the representations of Latino identities within the programs are historical, contradictory and complex, aiming for a nuanced, pluralistic view of Latino cultures is one way to move beyond stereotypes. At the same time, the programs present a nostalgic, glamorized depiction of Latino/as that has little to do with how Latino/as actually live and with who they might think they are.

Given these polar tendencies, the thoughtful IC instructor might decide that use of the videos is too risky. How does one teach cultural acceptance and interactional compatibility with an artifact that is so incredibly flawed? How does an instructor, after all, get past Andy Garcia telling Jimmy Smits that he will take Gloria Estefan offstage and "show her my bongos"?

Our solution returns to epideictic rhetoric. The instructor is a performer of values and a conductor of emphasis who can see the advantage to these polar tendencies. As Conquergood (1985) states of the cultural performance: "The strength of the center is that it pulls together mutually opposed energies that become destructive only when they are vented without the counterbalancing pull of their opposite" (p. 9). With this insight, we offer the following questions that might be helpful when considering Latino epideictic rhetoric in the IC course:

- What interpretations of Latino/a experiences are conveyed through this performance text? How do these interpretations cohere or contradict and what do these imply about Latino cultures?
- What does the performance text make possible for participants? What does the program allow the participants to do that is important to them?
- What are the distinctive ways that Latino/as amplify or magnify as they honor one another?
- What historical and political context have you provided for understanding and discussing struggles surrounding language, migration, education, class mobility, and inclusion in political and media systems?
- Are you prepared to discuss language loyalty and strategic bilingualism?
- What Latino/a cultural meanings appear to be renewed, (re)created, opposed, or preserved?
- What concepts are needed to understand the performance text from within its Latino/a sensibility?

For IC instructors as well as instructors who bring a cultural focus to other disciplines, these considerations are necessary if they are to address these issues in responsible and ethical ways. As a starting point, an IC instructor should ask her/himself these questions as a means of accessing their own preparedness in engaging with these materials. Another option is for the IC instructor to utilize several of these questions as springboards into class discussion upon viewing these award shows. Both options allow for an exploration and discussion of ethic identities that recognize the multifaceted nature of Latino identities and cultures. Being prepared for such as discussion, through exploring the above considerations should be the goal of an instructor who desires to bring this course content into their classrooms.

CONCLUSION

Like the creation of this journal, the Latino Grammys and the ALMA awards are responses to intense curiosity about Latinos and Latinas. The shows function as epideictic rhetoric because their primary purpose is to honor various film and musical artists and performers. As we have illustrated, the key strategies for amplification are expressions of unity and difference.

Educators also are implicated in epideictic since their work largely honors academic disciplines (just as in this article we honor communication studies) and their methods of discovery and analysis. In this sense, educators must examine the ways in which they are engaging in course materials within their fields of study. Part of this examination requires asking questions of ourselves as well as our students as a means of engaging this course content in responsible and ethical ways.

The use of Latino/a epideictic rhetoric in the IC classroom should be approached with an appreciation of history and a disregard for coherence. Latino/as as course content must never be finalized, but always must remain an open dialogue. It is our hope that we have provided an entry point for such dialogue.

REFERENCES

Anzaldúa, G. E. (2000). *Interviews/entrevistas*. New York: Routledge.

Aristotle. (1932). *The rhetoric* (L. Cooper, Trans.). Englewood Cliffs, NJ: Prentice-Hall.

Associated Press. (2000, September 13). *Fund-raising tactics for Latin Academy of Recording Arts & Science questioned*. Retrieved from http://web.lexisnexis.com/universe/doc...1&_md5= 31ca5ea4a22435e7e6dbla38e36c9a0c

Beltran, C. R. (2000, April 24). Counterpunch: Shows in Spanish also deserve ALMA notice. *Los Angeles Times*, p. F3.

Bianco, R. (1999, June 3). Critic's corner. *USA Today*, p. 12D.

Clark, N. (1996). The critical servant: An Isocratean contribution to critical rhetoric. *Quarterly Journal of Speech, 82*, 111–124.

Cobo, L. (2000, September 23). Latin Grammys have everyone talking. *Billboard*, 55–56.

Conquergood, D. (1985). Performing as a moral act: Ethical dimensions of the ethnography of performance. *Literature in Performance, 5*, 1–13.

Cossette, P. (Executive Producer). (2000, September 13). *First Annual Latin Grammy Awards*. New York: Columbia Broadcast System.

Delgado, C. F. (2000, September 21). Double cross: Is prime time really ready for Latin music? *Miami New Times*. Retrieved March 18, 2001, from http://web.lexisnexis.com/universe/doc...1&md5= f92126093e8f26c158f67222afad1381

Doss, Y. C. (1998, June 4). Latino awards battle stereotypes. *Los Angeles Times*, p. F47.

Ehrlich, K., & Yzaguirre, R. (Executive Producers). (2000, June 17). *The 2000 American Latino Media Arts Awards*. New York: American Broadcast Company.

Giroux, H. A. (1992). *Border crossings: Cultural workers and the politics of education*. New York: Routledge.

Kissell, R. (2000, Sept. 15). Latin Grammys bow with bland ratings. *Daily Variety*, p. 4.

Limón, J. E. (1998). *American encounters: Greater Mexico, the United States and the erotics of culture*. Boston: Beacon.

McKerrow, R. E. (1989). Critical rhetoric: Theory and praxis. *Communication Monographs, 56*, 91–111.

National Council of La Raza. (2000). Retrived March 20, 2001, from http://www.nclr.org.

Ocaña, D. (2000, November). Latin Grammys premiere: Will more Hispanic related shows appeal to a large audience? *Hispanic, 13,* 16.

Philips, C. (2000, September 13). Latin Grammy fund raising puts spotlight on academy; music industry: Proceeds from a $25,000-a-table benefit will not go to charity but to the group controlled by C. Michael Greene. *Los Angeles Times,* Financial Desk A1.

Poulakos, T. (1987). Isocrates' use of narrative in the Evagoras: Epideictic rhetoric and moral action. *Quarterly Journal of Speech, 73,* 317–328.

Sheard, C. M. (1996). The public value of epideictic rhetoric. *College English, 58,* 765–787.

Snow, S. (2000, September 29). Morning Report. *Los Angeles Times,* p. F2.

Valdes-Rodriguez, A. (1999, June 25). New Latin Grammys introduced. *Los Angeles Times,* p. F2.

Valdes-Rodriguez, A. (2000, August 30). Controversy over Latin Grammy nominees: Awards independent label claims academy shuns Mexican regional artists. *Los Angeles Times,* p. F3.

Werner, E. (2000, September 13). *Some artists boycott inaugaral Latin Grammys to protest perceived bias.* Retrieved March 12, 2001, from http://web.lexis-nexis.com/universe/doc...1&-smd5=468c5475fl9 d6d480df69f6fbl1e654b

JOURNAL OF LATINOS AND EDUCATION, 2(1), 59–65

U.S. Latino Audiences of "Telenovelas"

Diana I. Rios

*Department of Communication Sciences and
Puerto Rican and Latino Studies Institute
University of Connecticut, Storrs*

This audience response research focuses on Latino cultural-based experiences with television serial novels. I want to know why Latino audiences watch and what they get out of watching American soap operas and "telenovelas." Based on previous research Latinos' experiences with mass media is part of a cultural maintenance and assimilation process. That is, in various degrees, television serial novels may hold sociocultural value for U.S. Latinos, whether in English or Spanish. Latinos use melodramatic serials to keep in touch with Latino culture as well as learn more about and keep in touch with the dominant European American culture that surrounds them in their daily lives.

Key words: mass media, audiences, uses and gratifications, telenovelas, soap operas, Latinos, cultural maintenance, assimilation

Melodramatic serial novels in print or broadcast form, and by any other name, have long established themselves around the world as media for mass consumption (Allen, 1995). The success of "telenovelas"and soap operas in the United States points to the mass appeal of melodramas shown on television in the Americas. Latinos living in the United States, maybe as a result of immigration, U.S. territorial expansionism, or native birth, have maintained experiences with television serial novels in their daily lives. Whether individuals or families are consistent fans or not, the "telenovela" and soap opera habit continues to bring large advertising revenues to local television stations and national Spanish-language networks operating in the United States.

This study asks why Latino audiences watch, and what Latino audiences get out of watching television serial novels such as telenovelas and soap operas. Herzog (1944a, 1944b) conducted early research on why people listen to radio soap operas,

Requests for reprints should be sent to Diana I. Rios, Department of Communication Sciences/Puerto Rican & Latino Studies Institute, U–1085, University of Connecticut, Storrs, CT 06269. E-mail: diana.rios@uconn.edu

and many scholars since that time have been engaged in various types of "media uses and gratifications" research (Rosengren, Wenner, & Palmgreen, 1985; Webster & Phalen, 1997) and "audience-response" research (Bobo, 1995; Jhally & Lewis, 1992; Liebes & Katz, 1990; Press, 1991). The research also tries to identify dual processes of cultural maintenance and assimilation as part of media use (Rios, 2000; Rios & Gaines, 1997, 1998; Subervi-Velez, 1986). In various degrees, Latinos use melodramatic serials to keep in touch with Latino culture as well as learn more about and keep in touch with the dominant European American culture.

LATINO MEDIA USE: CULTURAL MAINTENANCE AND ASSIMILATION

The relationship that Latinos have with English-language and Spanish-language media is complex. A variety of studies have examined media use as part of Latino cultural processes (Faber & O'Guinn, 1986; Gutierrez & Schement, 1979; Rios, 1996, 1999; Rios & Gaines, 1997, 1998; Shoemaker, Reese, & Danielson, 1985; Soruco, 1996; Subervi-Velez, 1986; Warshauer, 1966). For example, Warshauer (1966) and Gutierrez and Schement (1979) examined broadcast media functions and consumer socialization. Warshauer (1966) states that although some media in Spanish may provide linguistic support, this can become incidental when the mother tongue is used on "behalf of commercial and 'Americanizing' goals" (p. 89). Gutierrez and Schement's (1979) research on Spanish-language radio in the southwest describes one radio station as emphasizing its "Mexicanness" but also "projecting American life in a language most acceptable to its listeners … as an agent of acculturation" (pp. 10–11).

Subervi-Velez (1986), Rios (1999, 2000), and Rios and Gaines (1997, 1998) explain that the role of mass media in Latino cultural maintenance (also called pluralism) is a process where individuals are exposed to ideas, information, and values that assist them in retaining Latino cultural values and group identification. Some media fortify Latino culture and provide cultural respite. Media use in the process of cultural level assimilation (acculturation) describes how media use can support cultural change toward dominant Anglo values and behavioral norms. Latinos may use media for selective acculturation to gain dominant cultural knowledge and learn cultural interaction and survival skills necessary in an Anglo American world. Media use in the process of structural level assimilation is a process where media can be used to gain access to social cliques and clubs controlled by the dominant culture and to gain opportunity to participate in economic and political structures of U.S. society.

Given the previous research on Latino audiences and mass media use, there is support to further examine the cultural-based reception of television serial novels.

METHODS AND DATA SOURCES

I have conducted interviews and focus group research with Latino audiences in the southwest and northeast during the past 10 years. This research reflects selected interviews that I gathered on a part time basis in greater Hartford, Connecticut, between 1999 and 2001. I used snowball sampling (Henry, 1990) to obtain a variety of volunteers who were members of the working and professional classes. Respondent ages range from late teens to late 60s. Eleven of the respondents were women and five were men. Pseudonyms are used. The types of work, ages, and ethnic country of origin are approximated to protect privacy.

I created a field guide that was composed of bilingual Spanish and English open-ended questions and some closed-ended questions. I took extensive notes during the interviews and showed respondents what I was writing. Interviews were conducted in English and Spanish, depending on respondent preferences and lasted about 1 hr. Interviews were conducted in people's homes, in a coffee shop, or at a cultural center at a college campus. In several cases, interviews were much longer and included follow-up interviews and contact in community activities and events in greater Hartford.

LATINOS RESPOND TO TELENOVELAS AND SOAP OPERAS

The cultural value of serials in the Latino community appears to be in contention, some finding that serials, especially in Spanish, provide the escape, entertainment, and cultural respite they need to deal with their daily lives. English-language serials may provide Latinos with escape, entertainment, and cultural information about Anglo society. There are also viewers that go along with others such as friends and family members because they want to spend time with and show respect, *respeto*, to family and cordiality, *simpatia*, to friends. Familism, respect for elders, respect for general traditions, and the maintenance of fictive kinship and interpersonal networks can be very important for Latinos. Serials, whether in Spanish or English can provide a means to fulfill cultural obligations; this is part of the cultural maintenance process.

Watching Novels to Maintain Family Ties

A young Connecticut professional woman named Mindy, in her 20s, explained how long she had been watching novelas and when she started, "all my life, since I was little. They have telenovelas from everywhere. They have a lot of different ones. I usually watched with my grandmother when I was about 6 years old." Here

Mindy valued the time she spent with her beloved grandmother. Watching serials was a way for her to maintain closeness and respect for grandmother's choice of television programming. Fortifying sociocultural glue among family members is of concern among Latinos.

Rob is a Puerto Rican male in his 20s. He was born in Puerto Rico but moved with his grandmother and other siblings to Connecticut. He currently works in an office with secretarial and professional duties in information management. He stated how he reluctantly watched novelas with family members, "from a baby to 11 years old, I would walk in, it was more involuntary," he states with an unhappy look on his face. Rob had a negative view of serials from a young age. He has tolerated serial novels out of respect for his mother and sister. Later, as an adult he tolerates them because his female and male friends watch them.

Nestor is a young businessman in his early 30s. He was born and raised in a small town in Puerto Rico and came to the mainland in the late 1980s. He was introduced to telenovelas by his sister, in Puerto Rico, who watched a great deal of them. The programs were a way for him and his sister to keep each other company. Nestor explained, "My sister watched many telenovelas. It's very common in Puerto Rico. When I was in seventh grade there was a Mexican telenovela called 'Los Ricos También Lloran.' I was in school and I would return at 1:00 p.m. and I watched with my sister." When he goes back to Puerto Rico to visit, he still watches telenovelas with his sister. By Nestor doing this, he not only exercises interest he has in novelas in his native tongue but he also maintains familial ties and demonstrates *respeto* to his older sister.

Selma is a middle-aged Puerto Rican secretary who was born and raised in Connecticut. She loves telenovelas for the purposes of entertainment and supporting familism. "There is nothing educational about them but I can relax. I watch them with my daughters and sometimes my husband." She has watched American soaps in the past but avoids them because of their content. She feels that they are less moral than novelas in Spanish, "The English telenovelas are a no-no. They should not be watched in front of little kids. *Days of Our Lives, Another World*, I used to watch 6 or 7 years ago."

Language and Culture Lessons

There are respondents who find that serials are useful for learning about the United States and for feeling connected with an ethnic homeland. Mrs. Tobias is an older retired South American woman who worked in the laundry and cleaning services. She openly discussed the acculturation (cultural assimilation) utility of English-language serials for her learning English and for learning about the people in her new country. Serials in English provided her a chance to mimic words and dialogue. Spanish-language serials, which came later with the availability of cable television and the growth of Spanish-language networks, offered her the warmth and comfort of her native language. Telenovelas, then, provided her a means for re-kindling cultural ties to the Latin America she left decades before. She also gained inspiration, and self-affirmation, from the Latina characters on the telenovelas who surmounted desperate situations and achieved a certain level of success.

Julius, a young professional, says he was drawn to English-language serials such as *Dynasty, Knots Landing, The Colbys,* and *Dallas* partically because they provided him with a cultural window of European America. He says "I was drawn to elegance, the attire, dress, use of English, and other [things] I found it in novelas in English not in Chicano novelas." He still kept a liking for Span-ish-language serials because of the relevance of some family topics, "Sometimes [we] would make analogies to family members; there was immediacy." Julius also recalled an anecdote that revealed how some audience members take serials too seriously. He did not want to be understood as an extreme viewer who would mistake a character for an actor. He explained that an actor who had played an antagonist in a novela was shunned by housekeeping staff in a big southwestern city, "she had gone to a hotel and the maid wouldn't clean her room because the maid punished her for the character she played on the novela." He eventually stopped keeping up so much with television serials because he "was tired of that life [on TV]. I had my own family. That's enough telenovelas for a day." But, interestingly enough, he has seen family members, such as his father, recently become truly hooked on telenovelas.

Protagonists as Role Models

Mrs. Tobias explains,

> When I lived in Hartford, I would watch the Spanish channels and the American ones. I watched the novelas *One Life to Live, All My Children*, and *General Hospital* since 1966. The novela was my English teacher. I didn't take classes. I wanted to learn the United States way of life and how people did things. During my breaks, I watched the American novelas and the Spanish novelas at night.

She goes on,

> It's therapy for me. It's therapy because I know I'm not the only one with problems. That I'm not alone. For example, *Rosa de Lejos* was about a poor girl that goes to a city from a small town … She falls in love and gets pregnant … when she told the father of the child, he disappears, he didn't want her … She sewed extremely well. She became a famous designer little by little. Her creations went all the way to France. Well, I'm not going to be a great designer but I don't need a man either to get ahead. I've had to work hard with two girls."

Voicing Dislike of Novelas

Not all respondents enjoy the television serial viewing experience, whether in English or Spanish. There were two respondents, in particular, who disliked serial novels, and also happened to be male. Rob has watched pieces of Spanish-language serials over the years and has never liked them. He explains, "Latin America is a diverse region. There are all kinds of people. The telenovela represents a small segmented part of society. It's fantasy-based reality and people get fooled into thinking that that's reality." In his opinion, telenovelas are harmful to society because "they perpetuate the Cinderella syndrome." He would prefer novelas to deal with "salt of the earth" types of people. He asks why female characters cannot be crafted differently in novelas, "What about a woman like the Phoenix who rises from the ashes and succeeds?" With regard to men who watch novelas, he believes that they might be just "going along with the crowd."

William, a young professional man who works in tourism, is in his mid-20s. He was born in Latin America and has lived in Connecticut for most of his life. He said, "I remember being a little kid and watching. I didn't like it. It made me feel bad for my aunt to be controlled by a TV show." He is critical about novela watchers saying that they give a bad reputation to those who watch other things on television, "I personally believe that novelas lead people to look down on TV watchers." He believes novelas can be disruptive in people's lives when fans create their schedules around novelas, "Some people schedule their classes [at school] around the soaps and telenovelas." He also is concerned that fans use novelas to displace real people in their lives, "When people concentrate on it, it's counterproductive. When people get over involved in the episodes, they think the characters are their friends and family." He acknowledges the entertainment and relaxation value of novelas for housewives and househusbands but he cautions fans "once it's over get back to reality. Use your break … but don't live there!"

CONCLUSION

Television serial novels are an expression of popular culture that will prevail in Latino communities in Connecticut. Depending on their needs or social place, Latinos may see melodramatic serials as tools to aid them in maintaining aspects of Latino culture (cultural maintenance) and learning more about or keeping in touch with the dominant European American culture (assimilation). Respondents may also have experiences or needs that do not fall neatly into a dual-culture dynamic of possibilities. Overall, Latinos' experiences with mass media are intertwined, although imperfectly, with cultural desires and needs. In future field research in the Latino community I look forward to a fuller examination of gender similarities and differences among respondents' experiences as well as possible in social class and generation differences and similarities.

REFERENCES

Allen, R. C. (1995). *To be continued ... soap operas around the world*. New York: Routledge.

Bobo, J. (1995). *Black women as cultural readers*. New York: Columbia University.

Faber, R. J., & O'Guinn, T. C. (1986). Diversity in the ethnic media audience: A study of Spanish-language broadcast preferences in the U.S. *International Journal of Intercultural Relations, 10*, 347–359.

Gutierrez, F. F., & Schement, J. R. (1979). *Spanish-language radio in the Southwestern United States*. Austin: University of Texas Center for Mexican American Studies.

Henry, G. T. (1990). *Practical sampling*. Newbury Park, CA: Sage.

Herzog, H. (1944a). Motivations and gratifications of daily serial listeners. In P. F. Lazarsfeld & F. N. Stanton (Eds.), *Radio research, 1942–1943*. New York: Duell, Sloan.

Herzog, H. (1944b). What do we really know about daytime serial listeners? In P. F. Lazarsfeld & F. N. Stanton (Eds.), *Radio research, 1942–1943* (pp. 3–33). New York: Duell, Sloan.

Jhally, S., & Lewis, J. (1992). *Enlightened racism*. Boulder, CO: Westview.

Liebes, T., & Katz, E. (1990). *The export of meaning: Cross-cultural readings of 'Dallas.'* New York: Oxford.

Press, A. (1991). *Women watching television: Gender, class and generation in the American television experience*. Philadelphia: University of Pennsylvania Press.

Rios, D. I. (1996). Chicano cultural resistance with mass media. In R. De Anda (Ed.), *Chicanas and Chicanos in contemporary society*. Boston: Allyn and Bacon.

Rios, D. I. (1999). Latina/o experiences with mediated communication. In A. Gonzalez, M. Houston, & V. Chen (Eds.), *Our voices*. Los Angeles: Roxbury.

Rios, D. I. (2000). Chicana/o and Latina/o gazing: Audiences of the mass media. In D. R. Maciel, I. D. Ortiz, & M. Herrera-Sobek (Eds.), *Chicano Renaissance: Contemporary cultural trends* (pp. 169–190). Tucson: University of Arizona Press.

Rios, D. I., & Gaines, S. O. (1997). Impact of gender and ethnic subgroup membership on Mexican Americans' use of mass media for cultural maintenance. *Howard Journal of Communications, 8*, 197–216.

Rios, D. I., & Gaines, S. (1998). Latino mass media use for cultural maintenance. *Journalism and Mass Communication Quarterly, 75*, 746–761.

Rosengren, K. E., Wenner, L. A., & Palmgreen, P. (1985). *Media gratifications research: Current perspectives*. Beverly Hills, CA: Sage.

Shoemaker, P., Reese, S. D., & Danielson, W. A. (1985). Spanish-language print media use as an indicataor of acculturation. *Journalism Quarterly, 62*, 734–740, 762.

Soruco, G. R. (1996). *Cubans and the mass media in South Florida*. Gainesville, FL: University Press.

Subervi-Velez, F. A. (1986). The mass media and ethnic assimilation and pluralism: A review and research proposal with a special focus on Hispanics. *Communication Research, 14*, 71–96.

Warshauer, M. E. (1966). Foreign language broadcasts. In J. Fishman (Ed.), *Language loyalty in the United States* (pp. 75–91). The Hague, The Netherlands: Mouton & Co.

Webster, J. G., & Phalen, P. F. (1997). *The mass audience: Rediscovering the dominant model*. Mahwah, NJ: Lawrence Erlbaum Associates, Inc.

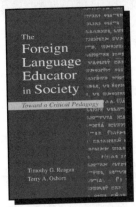

THE FOREIGN LANGUAGE EDUCATOR IN SOCIETY

Toward a Critical Pedagogy

Timothy G. Reagan
Terry A. Osborn

University of Connecticut

"A groundbreaking work in the field of foreign/second language pedagogy. The authors' innovative and brilliant analysis of the role of the foreign/second language educator in society...together with their perceptive discussion of the need for critical pedagogy provides a refreshing and constructive approach [that is] at the cutting edge of the field....It is unique in that it addresses essential curricular, methological, and pedagogical issues that have long been ignored by the profession....This textbook ought to be required reading for all students enrolled in a foreign language education program, as well as for foreign/second language instructors, for their supervisors, and for those administrators directly involved in curriculum development and assessment."

—**Frank Nuessel**
University of Louisville

This text brings together two significant domains of educational practice: foreign language education and critical pedagogy—linking them in a way that can help foreign language educators develop a critical awareness of the nature, purposes, and challenges facing foreign language pedagogy. Unique among texts in the field, this is the first to deal explicitly with the social, political, ideological, and economic aspects of language, language learning, and language teaching in our society and to connect the practice of foreign language education with these critical, and crucial, aspects of language and language use. *The Foreign Language Educator in Society: Toward A Critical Pedagogy:*

- emphasizes what teachers and future teachers of foreign languages in this country ought to know and understand about language— language attitudes, practices, rights, and policy— and related issues;
- focuses on helping students to move beyond pragmatic pedagogical concerns to the social and political concerns relevant to their teaching; and
- provides students with the opportunity to develop critical perspectives on the central facets of the language education process.

Intended for foreign language education programs at both basic and advanced levels, as well as courses in critical pedagogy, critical language awareness, sociolinguistics, and social and cultural foundations of education, the text provides helpful pedagogical features to direct the reader in applying the content of each chapter to his or her own context.

Contents: Preface. When Methodology Fails: A Critical Look at Foreign Language Education. From Reflective Practice to Emancipatory Knowledge in Foreign Language Education. Whose Language Is Real? Language Variation and Language Legitimacy. Constructivist Epistemology and Foreign Language Teaching and Learning. Critical Curriculum Development in the Foreign Language Classroom. Foreign Language Teaching as Social Activism. Language Rights as Human Rights: Social and Educational Implications. When in Rome (or Pretoria): Language Policy in International Perspective. Toward a Critical Foreign Language Pedagogy.
0-8058-3592-X [paper] / 2002 / 200pp. / $24.50
Prices are subject to change without notice.

Lawrence Erlbaum Associates, Inc.
10 Industrial Ave., Mahwah, NJ 07430–2262
201–258–2200; 1–800–926–6579; fax 201–760–3735
orders@erlbaum.com; www.erlbaum.com

SUBSCRIPTION ORDER FORM

Please ☐ enter ☐ renew my subscription to:

JOURNAL OF LATINOS AND EDUCATION

Volume 2, 2003, Quarterly — ISSN 1534–8431/Online ISSN 1532–771X

SUBSCRIPTION PRICES PER VOLUME:

Category:	Access Type:	Price: US/All Other Countries
☐ Individual	Online & Print	$40.00 / $70.00

Subscriptions are entered on a calendar-year basis only and must be paid in advance in U.S. currency—check, credit card, or money order. Prices for subscriptions include postage and handling. Journal prices expire 12/31/03. **NOTE:** Institutions must pay institutional rates. Individual subscription orders are welcome if prepaid by credit card or personal check. **Online access is included with individual subscriptions. Please note:** A $20.00 penalty will be charged against customers providing checks that must be returned for payment. This assessment will be made only in instances when problems in collecting funds are directly attributable to customer error.

☐ **Check Enclosed** (U.S. Currency Only) **Total Amount Enclosed $_____**

☐ **Charge My:** ☐ VISA ☐ MasterCard ☐ AMEX ☐ Discover

Card Number _____ Exp. Date_____/____

Signature_____
(Credit card orders cannot be processed without your signature.)
PRINT CLEARLY for proper delivery. STREET ADDRESS/SUITE/ROOM # REQUIRED FOR DELIVERY.

Name_____

Address_____

City/State/Zip+4_____

Daytime Phone #_____E-mail address_____
Prices are subject to change without notice.

For information about online subscriptions, visit our website at *www.erlbaum.com*

Mail orders to: **Lawrence Erlbaum Associates, Inc.,** Journal Subscription Department
10 Industrial Avenue, Mahwah, NJ 07430; **(201) 258–2200; FAX (201) 760–3735;** journals@erlbaum.com

LIBRARY RECOMMENDATION FORM

Detach and forward to your librarian.

☐ I have reviewed the description of the *Journal of Latinos and Education* and would like to recommend it for acquisition.

JOURNAL OF LATINOS AND EDUCATION

Volume 2, 2003, Quarterly — ISSN 1534–8431/Online ISSN 1532–771X

Category:	Access Type:	Price: US/All Other Countries
☐ Institutional	Online & Print	$195.00/$225.00
☐ Institutional	Online Only	$175.00/$175.00
☐ Institutional	Print Only	$175.00/$205.00

Name_____Title_____

Institution/Department_____

Address_____

E-mail Address_____
Librarians, please send your orders directly to LEA or contact from your subscription agent.

Lawrence Erlbaum Associates, Inc., Journal Subscription Department
10 Industrial Avenue, Mahwah, NJ 07430; **(201) 258–2200; FAX (201) 760–3735;** journals@erlbaum.com

LANGUAGE IDEOLOGIES

Critical Perspectives on the Official English Movement
Volume I: Education and the Social Implications
of Official Language
Volume II: History, Theory, and Policy
Edited by

Roseann Dueñas González
*University of Arizona, Tucson and National Center
for Interpretation Testing, Research, and Policy*
With

Ildikó Melis
University of Arizona, Tucson
Co-published with the National Council of Teachers of English

How do educators balance the rights of the rapidly growing percentage of the United States' population whose first language is not English or whose English differs from standard usage with the rights of the majority of students whose first and generally only language is English? This two-volume set addresses the complicated and divisive issues at the heart of the debate over language diversity and the English Only movement in U.S. public education. The book offers a wide range of perspectives that teachers and literacy advocates can use to inform practice, as well as policy. Both volumes explore the political, legislative, and social implications of language.

Lawrence Erlbaum Associates, Inc.
10 Industrial Ave., Mahwah, NJ 07430–2262
201–258–2200; 1–800–926–6579; fax 201–760–3735
orders@erlbaum.com; www.erlbaum.com